Henrik Monggaard Christensen – born in 1968, lieutenant commander in the Royal Danish Navy, trained at the Danish Air Force Flying School in Karup, tactical coordinator at Royal Danish Naval Air Squadron in Vaerloese and 723 Squadron in Karup 1997-2014, with more than 300 days in the Danish campaign against piracy in the western Arabian Sea 2008-2013. Today, he is working as staff officer in the Danish Naval Staff in Karup together with a PTSD diagnosis.

To my four miracles: Sofie, Laura, Gustav and Emil.

Henrik M. Christensen

PIRATE HUNTER

AUSTIN MACAULEY PUBLISHERS™

LONDON · CAMBRIDGE · NEW YORK · SHARJAH

A CIP catalogue record for this title is available from the British Library.

ISBN 9781035815043 (Paperback)
ISBN 9781035815050 (ePub e-book)

www.austinmacauley.co.uk

First Published 2024
Austin Macauley Publishers Ltd®
1 Canada Square
Canary Wharf
London
E14 5AA

Grateful thanks to my lovely and patient wife Lene. All the best to my ex wives. Many thanks to my old friend Graeme McCutheon, Call Sign 'Gordie/GUN'. Thanks to Royal Navy for a lot of combined training, exercise and operations – special thanks to 750, 702 & 815 Naval Air Squadrons.

Table of Contents

Hobro

Silkeborg   Aarhus

Karup

Vaerloese

Copenhagen

Jutland

Funen   Zealand

The Darkness

HDMS Iver Huitfeldt, April 30, 2013
Off Hobyo, Somalia

'Can you fly into the country and retrieve them?' the commanding officer shouted through the operations room.

He looked at MER, the helicopter pilot who had been summoned over the intercom.

'Yes,' MER replied promptly.

I stood next to him and felt the cold sweat all over my body. What did he say?

We're not going over land, are we?

The thoughts were racing through my head.

I had been present in the operations room for some time, following the development and it did not look good. There were disturbances in the area, intelligence showed.

Clan disputes.

The money had long been handed over and counted and the six hostages should be on their way to the beach according to the arrangement But, nothing happened. Nothing happened for hours. And now, rumours had it that there was trouble on land. Management feared that another clan or pirate group would try to kidnap the hostages. Or that they would get caught in crossfire.

'Can you fly into the country and retrieve them?' MER was cocksure.

Time was running out. The hostages would not be able to be handed over on the beach and time agreed upon.

The darkness was on its way.

1. All Systems Go

Nec Temere, Nec Timide
– neither rashly nor timidly!

Everything is more difficult at night.

I sat at the dining table in the house in Lyngby with a cup of coffee and looked at the letter from the Ministry of Defence.

Adventure had always been in my blood. As a child, I had swallowed up the stories *Treasure Island*, *Robinson Crusoe* and *The Children of the New Forest* over and over again. Eventually the pages of the books nearly crumbled between my fingers. When I became a bit older, I became a scout and I had felt a special joy in putting on the uniform and had often spent time silently admiring my dagger. All right, I had always needed to work up the nerve, pull myself together, when we fought in school or when we played football, and even later on when I became a soldier and we were doing training missions. But when everything was rolling, when it became serious, with no possibility of retreat, when you would reach the point where your eyes started stinging and the taste of metal in your mouth became almost unbearable, the point where everybody else gave up, I endured.

Then the adventure overshadowed my worries.

The cold war was going on when I joined the army in the late 1980s. We had trained to beat the Russians but no one at the barracks had thought that we would ever need our skills in reality.

When the Berlin Wall fell, we felt assured. We were, like our fathers before us, a generation of the Danish army that would never see combat.

Or so we thought.

Because now, about ten years later, at the beginning of a new millennium, on top of the Gulf War, the conflict in former Yugoslavia and, not least, the attacks on the US on 9/11, it all felt a bit warmer again.

The Ministry of Defence thought so too.

And now the suits in Parliament had asked us to decide whether or not we wanted to be deployed if Denmark were to become involved in a military action.

It was in early 2002 and I sat for a while and just stared at the letter.

Everything is more difficult at night.

The helicopter is standing on a darkened ship deck and you have to find your way out there and belt up, using only the red glow from your small flashlight to aid you. Open the left door, crawl inside, crawl into your seat. Attach the harnesses from your life vest to the seat, fasten the other harnesses to the helicopter, still without being able to see much of anything. Put on your helmet and connect to the internal communications system.

You sit there in your small tin box, lit only by the dashboard. It is dark outside.

You are in your own little world.

We begin with our individual checks. *FLIR off, compass variation set, IFF off.* And one page down through the checklist. *Radar controls fully anti-clockwise.*

We start up the two Rolls Royce turbine engines of the helicopter. The rotors start turning. We perform the last checks together.

Outside temperature plus 15, NAV light on, pitot heating off.

And one page further.

TDS fix / doppler on. Check. Take-off-check complete.

Then we call the ship's control unit on the radio. 'A1A, this is Brumbass. Request take-off.'

And the ship responds, 'This is A1A, you are cleared to take off. Relative wind red 30/40 knots. QNH 1018.'

'Cleared take-off, copied wind, QNH 1018, Brumbass out.'

We use the red flashlight to signal our Flight Deck Director. He sends out four ratings into the darkness. They remove the lashings that until now have secured our position on the ship's deck. At this point, the only thing holding us down is the helicopter's harpoon in the metal grid below us and the pressure from the rotors We let the harpoon release its grip in the grid, power up the rotor and hover a few metres above the deck while we do an after take-off-check.

Airborne.

Then we pull out over the port side of the ship, increasing acceleration and altitude.

Out in the bottomless night.
All systems go.

*

I was born on April 3, 1968, in a town in Jutland named Silkeborg. My father, Børge, was studying to be a teacher at the time. My mother, Aase, was employed in the medical insurance fund in town. We lived in a flat just outside the town. A few years later we got a flat above the insurance fund. I also got a brother, Jens, and a sister, Anne, and my father got a job teaching in Skanderborg. Then we moved again. When he was offered a position as headmaster at a school in Hobro, we moved north.

My parents have always been employed in the public sector and, all in all, I had an average Danish upbringing. I went to high school, I was bored and I signed up for military service afterwards.

The army regiment in Slagelse, Denmark's oldest from 1614. I knew from the beginning that I wanted to become an officer in the Danish defence. I had only expected to stay in the system for some years but before long, I was hooked. It was great to try something practical. It was great to learn something and find out that it also worked in reality. As my never really blossoming youth rebellion died down, I became more and more captivated with my father's stories. He had himself been a sergeant in the army like his father before him. For as long as I could remember, they had told stories of the honourable life in the military and the importance of a strong defence.

Soon they also began telling those same kinds of stories on television.

When Saddam Hussein's Iraq attacked Kuwait in September 1990, the United States immediately sent armed forces to the Gulf. The American efforts to gather a coalition that could support the retaliation were so successful that, when Operation Desert Storm began five months later, 12 countries had naval forces shipped out to assist the Americans. Admittedly, the Danish parliament decided that the Danish contribution, a naval corvette by the name of Olfert Fischer, was not to participate actively in armed actions. But it still had the faint smell of war and we were many from the barracks who had a hard time hiding our enthusiasm when my army platoon and I shortly thereafter visited the naval base on Holmen in Copenhagen.

Today, this old naval base is transferred to a civilian residential area and a museum exhibition of ships, but back then it was packed with torpedo boats, corvettes and submarines. We were taken inside to see the operations rooms of a corvette and a torpedo boat. The Ops-room, as they called it. It was from there, a war on water was managed. We had the opportunity to observe a training exercise where the senior officers ran around in their freshly pressed uniforms delegating orders, while the specially trained marines concentrated on following the developments on big screens in front of them. It was just like in the movies.

I was deeply fascinated and when we got home, I had no doubt about what I wanted to do with my career.

In mid-1991, I began my training at the Royal Danish Naval Academy on Holmen in Copenhagen. The school was built in the late 1930s but despite its impressive exterior, the modern yellow bricks and functional style, you still felt the institution's age of over 300 years from the moment you stepped into the hall. You also noticed the giant image of the naval hero Niels Juel and his motto: *Nec Temere, Nec Timide* – neither rashly nor timidly. As cadets we observed it with awe every morning when we rushed to muster in the big hall and gathered under the large mural depicting the Battle of Køge Bay 1677, where Niels Juel beat the Swedes. Indeed, the presence of history could be felt like a draught through the halls at the school, and we found it completely natural to combine our studies of navigation and marine engineering with dance training and the annual cadet ball.

Naval officers were required to have proper etiquette, the mantra said. We were the noblemen of the sea.

There were three roles in our work, they used to say in the school: the manager, the diplomat and the warrior.

This suited me well. I loved it.

But I also knew which of the three suited me the best.

*

'Cleared take-off, copied wind, QNH 1018, Brumbass out.'

We pull out over the port side of the ship and increase acceleration and altitude.

We perform the last check and report back to the ship.

All systems go.

It is a beautiful starry evening. We are moving north, up through Kattegat. Once again, it is time to check our equipment, our sensors and communication with the ship.

Our task is to find an opponent who is moving down towards our forces from the north.

It's like taking a fishing trip.

Our infrared night system, FLIR, works fine tonight, conditions are good. We can see in the dark but the opponent cannot see us.

We are the invisible ones.

There is a blip on the radar and we detect a target, which, I see, is located somewhere near the island Anholt. And now, the pilot and the technician report a visual ship light somewhere ahead of us.

The heart rate slightly increases. The jaw closes and a couple of sweat droplets emerge.

The fish touches the line.

*

On a summer's day in 1995, I was appointed first lieutenant. With speeches and drum corps. After my education and training, I worked, among other things, as a fisheries officer in the North Atlantic. There I became acquainted with some of the Navy helicopters, and it made a great impression on me to see them in action.

As a naval officer it was possible to become a helicopter pilot in the Naval Air Squadron in Værløse air base, I found out, and it did not take long before I had signed up for the entrance examination.

The test consisted of multiple elements, ranging from mathematical tasks to practical challenges, for instance where you had to sit and press some buttons every time a lamp would go on in order to show that you could multitask.

We also had to go through a conversation with a psychologist who constantly interrupted with annoying questions.

'Where did you say you were from? Silkeborg? Try and spell that backwards, would you?'

Then you would sit there and turn the letters around in your head, while he started drumming his pen on the desk. At the same time, you had to follow a track with two pencils on a piece of paper, following the rhythm. All to test your stress level and multi-tasking capability.

There were no physical tests. The school counted on you as a soldier to have that part in order. We did, however, need to take a trip to hospital to have our vision examined. Those who used glasses or contact lenses were dumped on the spot, no matter how qualified they otherwise were. We were also measured and weighed but that was less important. Those who applied as fighter pilots were not allowed to be too tall because then their legs might get caught and severed in case they had to shoot themselves off using the ejection seat, we were told.

We did not have that problem.

'There is no ejection seat in a helicopter. If you need to think about why that is, then this job might not be right for you after all,' the examination leader said.

A military leader must always make sure that he or she has complete overview of a situation. This, in order to make optimal decisions.

A leader on the ground will want to know what type of activity there is in the terrain. He will send a unit ahead to clear the area. It can be a small group in a small vehicle with some binoculars and a radio, so they can report back what they see.

A naval commander with a naval force on the sea will very much want to know of other ships in his area. He will want an image of where the opponents are and what the naval traffic holds of merchant ships, fishing boats, ferries and pleasure crafts. The Danish naval force consists of five ships.

A frigate is equipped with radars, cannons, missiles, communication equipment and a helicopter. The helicopter is an ISR platform – Intelligence, Surveillance and Reconnaissance platform with sensors and communication equipment just like a reconnaissance vehicle on the ground. And the helicopter is extremely effective for that mission. From the air a helicopter can relatively quickly gain overview of a large area of the sea.

For many years we have had eight Westland Lynx helicopters in Denmark. The Dansh Lynx helicopter is a small blue workhorse which has earned its keep, especially by solving rescue and fishing inspection tasks in the North Atlantic.

But the Lynx can also be used in war.

Its crew mostly consists of a technician in the back of the cabin, a pilot in the right seat and a tactical coordinator in the seat on the left.

The tactical coordinator, or TACCO, as he is also called, is there to make sure that the helicopter is in the right place at the right time. In NATO terms this function is also called mission commander. It is a task that requires both great preparation before a mission and attention during the mission itself. Here, the tactical coordinator has to perform regular co-piloting work like navigation, fuel calculations and maintenance of communication with the ship's air traffic control, he must maintain the tactical overview, operate the radar and communicate with other armed forces and he needs to make sure the helicopter points in the direction of the enemy and point out any possible targets.

The tactical coordinator is able to take over the steering and land the helicopter if necessary. If, for instance, the pilot is shot. A helicopter is steered with a stick. It mostly resembles a joystick for a computer, and there is one located in each side of the helicopter, so you do not have to pull out the body of the pilot in order to take over the control.

However, said plainly, it is the guy on the right who flies the helicopter and the guy on the left who has the overview and controls the communication and points out where to direct fire.

The job as the guy on the left became my career and my destiny.

Both the training and the work as TACCO-student took place at the air force base in Værløse and this suited me fine. I had met my first wife while training to be an officer, and since it was not a requirement to live at the air force base, we moved in together.

Her name was Marianne. We got married in 1995 and in 1996, while I was still in training, she gave birth to our first daughter, Sofie. And in 2001 Laura was born. Shortly after, we all moved into an old brick villa in Lyngby. Marianne got the garden she had wanted, and I was allowed to hang my painting of the *Battle of Heligoland* in the living room.

*

All systems running.

I put the radar measurements into the TDS and link them home to our mother ship. TDS. Tactical Data System.

An image of a merchant ship appears on the FLIR. FLIR. Forward Looking Infra-Red.

No enemy, no danger. Yet.

We pass over the merchant ship, which is southbound in the Tango shipping route, and cannot see any more targets in front of us. Our enemy is hiding in the dark, where he theoretically is able to hit us with his surface-to-air missiles.

The darkness and the sound of the engine surround us for a minute's time. I sit slightly restless in my seat. Then a silhouette slowly appears on the FLIR. It is a naval ship. I give the pilot a nod. We report back to our mother ship. A clear image of a Standard Flex with a cannon on the front deck appears.

The fish is on the hook.

We are out of reach of arms, its pointed teeth cannot touch us while updating the target's coordinates and sending them back to our ship so they can launch a surface-to-surface missile.

Fortunately, it is just a training exercise this time.

We are located north of Anholt when our mother ship simulates the attack and the first part of the task is solved. Now we have to get back and land before the tank is empty. I see that we have enough fuel to stay in the area for about ten more minutes. The latest update from our own ship shows us that it is headed north, passing the northwest headland of Zealand. Beautiful evening. Making it won't be a problem. Then a text message arrives from the ship.

'Helo control, radar down.'

They are pretending to have a broken radar. We have to perform an HCA, a helicopter-controlled *approach,* where I as tactical coordinator have to instruct the pilot in doing a night landing on the ship. I programme the TDS to the HCA, and soon after we are at an altitude of 400 feet with a speed of 100 knots.

'Approach course 050.'

The ship is three nautical miles ahead of us.

'At the gate, reduce to 60 knots, left 5 heading 045. 1.5 stand by to descend. 1.2 start descend. Left 5, 040. one mile check 350. Three quarters of a mile, check 275, half-a-mile check 200 right 5, 045, quarter of a mile check 125 look up for sight.'

We are hovering above the port side of the ship. The sea is flat tonight. We receive landing permission and a green light, we slide in over the bright helicopter deck and put the helicopter down in its place.

Bump.

It's a good thing that the landing gear on a Lynx is sturdy enough to be dropped down from ten feet without damaging the helicopter.

When the rotor is turned off, I turn to the pilot and give him thumbs up. He smiles, we laugh but we both know that something is hiding behind his otherwise satisfied expression.

We both share the same dream and wish that it wasn't just a training exercise.

Everything is truly more difficult at night. But some decisions are easy to make, whether it is light or dark.

The day I received the letter from the Ministry of Defence about the possibility of deployment for military missions in foreign countries, I had no doubt.

I glanced at the picture of *the Battle of Heligoland*, emptied the coffee cup and signed.

2. The Way to Somalia

The trip is going to be nice and easy.
I am sure of it.

'We were about 210 nautical miles from the Somali coast when the hijacking took place. The hijackers sailed in three small boats that were not detected by the ship's radar and there were no large ships in the vicinity. Even if we had detected them, we would not be able to escape them at all. The current was against us and we were travelling at five or six knots.'

I sat in the office in Karup and read the newspaper. It was September 2007. Three years earlier, all of the military's helicopters had been moved to the airbase in Jutland and I was now part of what was called Helicopter Wing Karup, the naval helicopter service.

It was a bit like my old Asterix comics. We were a village of Gauls, we used to say jokingly. For we were still part of the Navy with all its pomp and splendour and gentleman ship but officially we had become squadron in the Air Force with all its testosterone and arrogance.

They were crazy, those Romans, we said to each other.

Well, I sat in my office reading the newspaper.

Three months earlier, the Danish merchant ship Danica White had been hijacked in the waters off the coast of Somalia. By pirates.

'Even if we had detected them, we wouldn't be able to escape them,' the captain said.

I took a sip of the lukewarm, slightly bitter coffee which I had retrieved from the vending machine five minutes earlier. My colleague Harry had also been there to get a cup for himself. We had talked about his new kayak, about the pirates in Somalia and about what the difference between a latte and a cappuccino was. I had hurried back and unfolded the newspaper.

I did not care about the latte and the cappuccino but...pirates!

Just reading the word was strange enough in itself. My thoughts went back to *Treasure Island* and Long John Silver with his wooden leg, scimitar and a parrot on the shoulder. Who drank rum straight from the bottle and put an X on a map when he had buried a treasure.

I read in the newspaper that there had been five Danish mariners on-board Danica White. Captain Niels H. Nielsen, a navigator, an experienced sailor and two inexperienced mariners, one was 21 and the other 18 years old.

The ship had been on its way from Dubai to Mombasa in Kenya when the pirates made their move.

'I was standing on the bridge of the ship doing a bunch of paperwork and sending home a telex with our position to the shipping company. I can't remember whether or not I was able to send it on time. Suddenly I heard yelling and screaming but I thought it was the two youngest crew members joking around. After that, I heard some loud bangs but I thought it came from supersonic aircrafts. But then there were more bangs and all of the sudden they were standing outside the door to the bridge, pulling and tearing at the door,' captain Niels H. Nielsen continued to explain to the newspaper.

The ship had been 210 nautical miles from the coast when the hijacking took place. That would be...almost 400 kilometres.

388, the calculator corrected me.

The captain had pushed the so-called pirate-button the minute he sensed danger, he said. However, the alarm that was supposed to go off at Naval Command Denmark apparently had not been working properly. Regardless, NCD, as we called them, did not hear anything about the whole thing, until the shipping company themselves made an alarm call to them.

Throwing a ladder up and over the railing of the ship and crawling onboard, had been a piece of cake for the 12–15 pirates.

'They separated the whites and the coloured. The coloured ones were just considered niggers and were thrown into the hold. Then there was only one door that needed to be kept locked. The rest of us were treated a little nicer because we were the ones worth money. Yeah, well, they weren't exactly nice all of the time. There was commotion at times and they threatened with machineguns. There were some really harsh types. There was one in particular, a real brute. Hell, nobody liked him. They yelled and screamed and threatened us,' Niels H. Nielsen told the newspaper B.T., when the drama had finally ended.

It had lasted for 83 days.

83 days where the American war ship USS Carter Hall had tried to stop the Danica White, among other things by blowing up the two smaller boats the pirates were towing after the ship. It had not helped. Apparently, the Danish authorities had not done anything except aiding the shipping company H. Folmer & Co. with counselling in the negotiation process to free the hostages and the ship. The ransom was set at 723,000 dollars, about 3.4 million Danish crowns.

Whether or not this was a good result was not for me to say. Never before had Danish sailors been taken as hostages.

It was, of course, a success that all five crew members had gotten out alive.

Nonetheless, the psychological pressure had undoubtedly been terrible.

'We had negotiated back and forth with the shipping company in Denmark who had hired a former frogman-soldier from the Royal Danish Navy as negotiator. He kept saying that there was no money, so, finally, we believed that there was none,' Niels H. Nielsen told the newspaper B.T.

When the pirates left the ship after 83 days, he and the four other crew members had been picked up by a French navy vessel.

I drank the last coffee from my plastic cup and quivered at the thought of what those men had been through. It frustrated me that the Danish efforts had been limited solely to sitting in an office and talking on the phone.

Six years ago, I signed a statement saying that I would gladly go on missions abroad. But I had not done much else than sitting in an office ever since.

The Somali pirates were not like the ones in Treasure Island. No wooden legs, eye patches or parrots on the shoulders.

Also, their story was not as colourful as the ones I had read as a boy.

Since the dictator Mohamed Siad Barre was overthrown in 1991, Somalia had been chaos. The breakdown and the confusion after the coup had thrown the East African country into a chaotic civil war, where clans and tribes fought against each other. The United Nations sent relief aid, but it was stolen, and in 1992, US President George Bush decided to place troops in the country to help restore peace.

With a feeling of horror, most of us at Karup Air Base remembered the images of the two Black Hawk helicopters that were shot down over the capital Mogadishu by Somali militia who afterwards dragged the bodies of the pilots triumphantly through the city.

Bloody hell.

Somalia had already been in a poor condition but after the state's collapse, things had looked even worse. Now there were not even a real police force to maintain discipline and order or any kind of coast guard controlling the country's coastline with a length of 3,300 kilometres. The lack of control had attracted foreign fishing boats that took advantage of the chaos on land to empty the ocean of tuna and lobsters. This had been one of the world's richest seas, however, now, the approximately 60,000 Somali fishermen felt that the foreign ships pushed them away and made their existence even more miserable than it already was. The fishermen had started to rebel against the development and the anger and poverty had developed into piracy.

It had been like this for over ten years.

The stories of modern pirates were well-known, also in Denmark. Although, they had never been this ruthless. In 2004, seven attacks and hijackings carried out by Somali pirates were verified. The following year the number was 48.

The negative development, they said, was blamed especially on Somali businessman Mohamed Abdi Hassan. He had founded the Hobyo-Harardhere Piracy Network and convinced other African businessmen to invest in the industry. In boats, in weapons and in crew. In only a few years, Mohamed Abdi Hassan's group of pirates, who operated under the name Somali Marines, had turned the otherwise anarchistic world of pirates into a professional industry.

The hijacking of Danica White was significant for the modern pirate industry.

200 years ago, when the first pirates scourged the Caribbean and off the eastern coast of Africa, the target was the cargo of the ship. It had been like this ever since, also for a period in time when especially Asian pirates threatened the merchant ships in the South China Sea throughout the '90s. But the pirates from Somalia were not after the cargo, no matter its worth. According to intelligence, Danica White had been transporting weapons, but even that did not interest the Somalis. They simply did not have the proper business network behind them who would be able to resell the ship's merchandise. The old Somali fishing ports had no cranes that could lift containers off the ships, and the poor infrastructure in Somalia meant that it would be impossible to get the goods transported any further. The Somali pirates were therefore

only interested in getting their hands on one thing. Cash. Ransom for the ship and for the people on it.

Not even six months went by, before it happened again. On February 1, 2008, almost a dozen armed Somali men crawled aboard the Danish-Russian tugboat Svitzer Korsakov sailing in the Gulf of Aden. 46 days went by before the six members of the crew were free again. The owners paid a ransom of 700,000 dollars, approximately 3.3 million Danish crowns.

This also made the Danish politicians run out of patience.

Back home in the old brick villa in Lyngby, we had run out of patience as well. Marianne was not particularly content with the fact that I often slept at the airbase instead of travelling back and forth every day and we had been getting on each other's nerves for a while.

She also thought I drank too much. She was right about that but I did not realise it until many years later.

One day, she insisted we get a new kitchen I refused. Why on earth would we want to do that? We already had a new bathroom. We began to quarrel and before the day was over, I had split.

All I took with me was the painting of *The Battle of Heligoland* and my DVD box set with *Das Boot*.

The adventurous spirit in me, which originally made me enlist into the Navy, was still alive when the Danish parliament in the late summer of 2008 decided that Denmark was to contribute to the international efforts against piracy. So, I was almost ecstatic when I was told I was to be part of it.

In the meantime I had moved in with my new girlfriend, Lisa, who I had met while being employed for at time at the

Royal Danish Defence College. She had a flat in Toldbodgade in downtown Copenhagen, really close to Nyhavn – a lively and bustling area in the old part of the city. Lisa was a psychologist student when I met her. Of course, the new love made it difficult for me to leave but Lisa insisted that I did not miss out on this experience.

The Danish contribution to the efforts against piracy initially consisted of the ship Absalon. The ship was supposed to help monitor the Gulf of Aden – the pirate-filled waters north of Somalia. Absalon was a 137-metre-long warship with bunks for 165 crew members and, of more importance for me, space for taking off and landing in a helicopter.

On August 17, 2008, the ship sailed out with a course set for the Horn of Africa where, one month later, it joined NATO's Task Force 150 which the coalition of warships was called. For a longer period of time, these joint forces had been present near the Horn of Africa, monitoring the trafficking of narcotics and weapons which especially the terrorist organisation Al-Qaida smuggled from Pakistan and further west through the Suez Canal and into Europe. However, from 2008, the task force directed their focus from weapons and narcotics onto protecting the area's merchant ships from pirates.

There had been 60 hijackings in the first half of 2008, we were told. That was 10 each month, one every three days. Over a short period of time the coast of Somalia had been plastered with permanent pirate camps by which the hijacked ships were anchored. At any given time there were about 30 hijacked ships lying off the coast. Every time someone was ransomed, new ones would just arrive.

The hostages were usually held trapped in the cargo holds of the ships.

Primarily, our task was to prevent more ships from being hijacked. For that purpose Absalon was equipped with both a Lynx helicopter and the Navy's fast rigid-hulled inflatable boats, or just RHIBs in daily speech.

Moreover, extra personnel were added to the ship's crew. In addition to our helicopter crew, these were intelligence officers, military police, computer experts, interpreters, a couple of doctors and nurses and then a team of elite soldiers from the Frogman Corps who, on the occasion of this mission operated under the more anonymous name SMTF.

The Special Maritime Task Force.

Our role in the helicopter was primarily to patrol the waters off Somalia, find the pirates and hopefully scare them away before they attacked a merchant ship. If the pirates succeeded in boarding a ship, it was our job in cooperation with the frogmen in their boats to make sure that the pirates gave up on their venture. For that same reason, we were permanently accompanied by one of the frogmen in our helicopter. His task was to operate a sniper rifle.

In daily speech, we just referred to him as the *sniper*. He was, for instance, able to shoot directly at the pirate's engines but if a pirate pointed their gun directly at the helicopter or the frogmen, he could also take them out with a precise shot. All of this while hanging in the air above the water. We were not supposed to land the helicopter at any time.

This was the general rule.

I was drafted to be part of the other helicopter crew who were going to the Gulf of Aden. It was a two-year posting, we were told and even before parliament had adopted the proposal we started training for the mission.

*

There is a big difference between taking off and landing a helicopter on land and on a ship. In bad weather a ship will rock, it is often dark and you have to be extremely careful that you do not fall into the water. The hardest part is landing. We like it best when the wind sweeps over the deck from the port side, so the ship is at full speed.

In average every ninth wave is smaller than the others, I learned at the school. I do not know if it is true but I used to always sit and count when we were approaching the deck.

Denmark had a total of nine ships from which it was possible to land and take off in a helicopter, so this part of the job was not new to us. We had been on several NATO drills in different locations, and on our annual trip to Scotland we practiced this part of our training. But we had never trained to be part of a pirate task force.

In a war situation, the most optimal thing a TACCO can do is to direct missiles straight into the face of the enemy to detect and report. To communicate. Report back what he sees.

It is a stressful situation while our friends on the warship can stay 75 nautical miles behind us and fire missiles without being seen, we are quite easily detected by the enemy. To put it blatantly, we train again and again in finding the enemy and directing some missiles straight into their face before they find us. We train in being invisible.

In a standard war situation our helicopter is manned by a pilot, a TACCO and a technician who can repair any

37

damages to the helicopter may suffer during battle.

But the situation in Somalia was different. We were not to direct missiles at the pirates. On the contrary we had to be ready to fly really close to them if it became necessary and thus, we had the need to be able to both attack and protect ourselves. Therefore, the Lynx in Somalia was not only equipped with a sniper from the Frogman Corps but also with a heavy machine gun which the technician learned to operate. We did not need a machine like this in war because if we did come close enough to be able to shoot the enemy into small pieces, they would have already shot us down. In a war situation our tactic was to stay so far away that the enemy could not reach us with their air missiles.

We called this distance "the stand-off distance" and it was an important principle in warfare from a helicopter.

And now we had to break this principle.

The machinegun was primarily used to shoot in the water around the pirate's boats in order to scare them or to shoot directly at the boats if the first move did not make them stop.

Much of our training before departure took place at the headland of Zealand where we looked for fishing boats. Subsequently, we fired warning shots at these large floating targets that had drifted off to sea to simulate stopping the boats.

One of the challenges was that we had to get really close because a small wooden ship can be hard to detect on our radar. Unfortunately, small wooden ships were the preferred transportation vessel of the Somali pirates.

The approach used by Mohamed Abdi Hassan's pirates was almost always the same: They stayed on so-called mother ships. This way the pirates could operate further from the coast and expand their hunting grounds further than they would be able to if they had to launch small boats directly from the shore. The mothership was most often a *dhow*, an Arabic wooden boat with a small wheelhouse and cargo hold. A boat like that is difficult enough to locate as it is. But when the attack began the pirates typically jumped into some even smaller but faster dinghies with outboard motors that were in tow of the dhow.

A skiff, they called this type of dinghy.

And it had happened exactly like this on that summer's day when Niels Nielsen and Danica White was hijacked.

In addition to the typical attack situations, we also trained something called fast-roping with the guys from the Frogman Corps. Fast-roping is when the frogmen slide down a rope hanging from the helicopter and they needed to have the opportunity to do this if we had to get aboard a ship and could not do so from the water. We also trained first aid so that we could take care of each other's injuries, as well as our own, if we were to get hit by incoming fire and had no possibility of getting back to the ship. Among other things, we practiced how to insert a plastic tube in through the nose, a so-called nasopharyngeal airway, in the event that our whole face was shot to pieces, making it impossible for us to breathe in the normal way.

Admittedly, there were moments where you considered, if sitting in the office at Karup airbase drinking vending machine coffee the rest of your days was in reality a better option.

Finally, we also trained with the frogmen in what to do, if we were shot down and taken as hostages. No one really wanted to talk about the risk but we all knew that it was a necessary scenario to prepare for. We were not the only ones who had seen the pictures of the American crew from the Black Hawk helicopters being dragged around the streets of Mogadishu.

When I was set to go on an INTOPS, I was usually charged several days before.

INTOPS. International Operation.

I will admit, I was a little insecure of the unknown and felt slightly discomforted by the situation and I really just wanted to throw myself into it and get it over with. Get things demystified. So, I was probably not the easiest person to deal with during those days halfway through 2008 and it was probably a relief for Lisa when she said goodbye to me and my colleagues in Karup Airport. It was strange waving at her through the glass window and knowing that we would not see each other for two months.

Lisa knew what I was getting into and she know the risks. Together we had been to a next of kin-event arranged by the Danish Defence. Here, families of deployed soldiers could hear about the mission and a friendly psychologist briefed us all about the relationship challenges you experience when being apart in two so different worlds.

In addition to the intelligence we had already received about the country, they also told us about Somalia in a more general but not less terrifying way. Lisa also did her own reading about the country with its almost 10 million inhabitants and their longstanding challenges and she could not help but notice the stories of Al-Shabaab especially. An extremely fundamentalist, Muslim terrorist organisation that later became a part of Al-Qaeda and who at the time had just started showing its teeth. Al-Shabaab did not kidnap

Westerners for the sake of money but to kill them it was said,
'You don't want to get caught by those people,' Lisa exhorted.

'Don't worry,' I said.

'The trip is going to be nice and easy. I'm sure of it,' I added that day at the airport before grabbing my bag, putting my hand on my heart and winked at her.

She knew that I was lying.

3. My Last Will

Funeral feast in the vicinity of Silkeborg.
The drinks are on me!

Dearest Sofie and Laura.

Sadly, I am dead now. But I will live on in your memories of the good times we've had together. It is okay to cry – it is totally fine and completely natural. Your mother and I loved each other when you two were created – you are love children. Give my best to her.

I did not get any further before I stopped. It was shortly before I went to the Gulf of Aden for the first time and I sat at the office in Karup and wrote farewell letters. It was part of the system, a requirement or at least an expectation that we actively considered how we would like to be buried, how our tombstones should look and those kinds of things in case we did not return. It was also expected that we wrote something personal to those closest to us.

We had been given a small dark red A5 booklet for the purpose. 'My last will,' it said on the front of the 14 pages. 'If I die in the line of duty,' it said beneath it.

Half of the booklet was already completed. We just had to do the rest. Make it personal.

I opened it on the first page and wrote my name and address. 'At my death, the following people must be contacted,' it said below.

I wrote Lisa's name, address and phone number. 'Relationship,' it said below.

'Girlfriend,' I wrote.

I also wrote my mother's name, Aase, on there. Relationship: Mother.

Unfortunately, my father had passed away in 1988.

On the dashed lines of the next pages, I wrote down who I would prefer to pass on the news of my death to those closest to me. Then I filled in the details of my funeral.

I want the funeral to take place: In church. Church of Our Lady, Silkeborg. My coffin/urn must be buried at: The western cemetery in Silkeborg.

Not only was I born in Silkeborg. But recently, I had also moved closer to my childhood town. While the girls lived with their mother in Copenhagen, Lisa and I moved into a small house in Them. Lisa had also gotten a job in Herning. Then none of us had to travel far to work.

'I am a member of a religious community,' it also said with a colon afterwards.

'Roman Catholic,' I wrote.

Our new little house lay far out in a forest. We still had the apartment in Nyhavn and I liked the big city but there was something special about living far out in the wilderness. Especially when you had just gone through a difficult divorce. There was tranquillity there were no officers shouting and there was no wife complaining. There was just me and her.

Lisa thinks it was during that period I started to look for answers to some of the more existential questions in life. But it had actually started before. However, it is true that my curiosity about spiritual things was aroused by her. Made me try to figure out how things are connected and whether there is any meaning to it all. I had always been interested in history and fascinated by the Catholic Church with all its art, its mystery and its clear division of good and evil. And I gradually found out that the pressure of my job was easier to cope with when I had something bigger to lean on.

When the big boss was with me at work.

The Catholic faith suited me well. So, I had converted and I had started praying. Yes, I even considered hanging a rosary in the helicopter but dropped it because it could quickly become dangerous if it broke and all the beads fell under the pedals.

I flipped a page in the small booklet and ticked off that I wanted a military funeral.

Decoration of the coffin? The Danish national flag. Check.

Hat.

Check.

Medals.

Check.

Sabre/dagger.

I put a line over dagger and ticked sabre.

I had had a sabre since training to be an officer and although I did not use it for anything, I felt it was an important part of my identity.

I want these flowers to be part of the decoration. Yellow + orange. Those were nice colours, I thought.

I want these songs/hymns to be sung:

On your way! Be brave and true!

Op al den ting, som Gud har gjort. Oh day full of grace.
Ora Pro Nobis.

'Special wishes for my dress in the coffin: Uniform. If possible,' I added.

There was no reason why Lisa or the undertaker should have to deal with the trouble of dressing me if I had been shot to pieces.

None of the exercises I had ever been on had been as difficult as it was filling out that small booklet. Training exercises were tangible. There you learned some theory and trained it in practice.

Learn some procedures or read them in a checklist. 'Yes, sir. Perform them. Yes, sir.'

We soldiers are good at that. We focus on the task and solve it.

Filling out your last will was also a task – an important task because it could make it easier for your loved ones to get through the grief if the practical things were in place. But it was not a task with the type of goal you felt achieved to accomplish.

It is hard to imagine being dead. I tried picturing my own funeral, both where I lay in the coffin and where I stood among the mourners. It was hard to imagine Lisa and the girls standing there and being ever so sad. Not being able to hold them and say that everything would be all right.

I shook off the worst melancholy and flipped one page over and filled in my insurance details and wrote where the insurance policy was stored.

'In the white shelving system, Lisa knows where,' I wrote.

Then I put down the six names of the ones I wanted to carry the coffin and ended up at the point about what should happen after the burial.

'Funeral feast in the vicinity of Silkeborg,' I wrote and added, 'The drinks are on me!'

Filling out the booklet was hard. But it was nothing compared to the pain and suffering that went into writing the accompanying farewell letters.

I wrote one to my mother before I finished the one for Sofie and Laura.

Dearest Mum.

Damn it! I am dead! Too bad, I was just getting my act together. I'm not here anymore but I still love you.

I really think we had a lot of good times together, especially within the last couple of years. I forgive you and Dad for the way you separated.

Enjoy the rest of your life, be good to yourself and your values. I know I live on in your memories and who knows, maybe we will meet again on the other side?

Give my best to Ole. The same goes for Jens and Anne and their children. Tell Jakob that I am in heaven. Give my best to the rest of the family.

I will keep an eye on you and take care of you all. I will say hi to Grandma and Grandpa for you. Ask the Virgin Mary to pray for me.

I will be buried from the Church of Our Lady, Silkeborg. I have filled in a booklet with details.

Tell Sofie and Laura how much I love them and how proud I am of them. I don't think I have lived in vain but that I have made my own little mark on this earth.

Sincerely,
Your son Henrik

I took two of the envelopes we had been given and put the letter to my mother in one, and the letter to my daughters in the other.

'This envelope contains my farewell letter.' (Was pre-printed with red letters on the front.)

I stamped one, wrote 'Mum' as the recipient and listed my name as the sender. I stamped it the other, wrote 'Laura and Sofie' as the recipients and listed my name as the sender.

'Dad,' I added below. Then I started crying.

Dearest Sofie and Laura.

Sadly, I am dead now. But I will live on in your memories of the good times we've had together. It is okay to cry – it is totally fine and completely natural. Your mother and I loved each other when you two were created – you are love, children. Give my best to her.

You will inherit some money from me when you become adults. Lisa and Grandma will be managing this money until then. However, keep in mind that money is not the most important thing in life. Being good to yourself and others is.

I love you, my two beautiful girls. I have been so proud of you and all the things you are good at. Both things you have in common but also areas where you each have shown your own strengths. Laura, you are so good in school, at sports and using your body actively. Sofie, you are a small adult person and very intelligent.

Enjoy life, it is a gift. Perhaps we will meet again in many years on the other side in heaven. Until then, cultivate wisdom, justice, courage and moderation.

I would like to ask you to do the following:

- *Get an education.*
- *Treat other people the way you wish to be treated by them.*
- *Think of me every now and then.*

I will keep an eye on you and take care of you from where I am now. Do not forget your dad and his family. Deep down, they are all right, those Jutes.

Ask the Virgin Mary to pray for me. Many endless, loving kisses and hugs.

Your dad,
Henrik.

I needed a break. Some air or just someone to talk to. I went down to the break room and allowed myself a cup of coffee with both milk and sugar from the machine. Harry, who was always ready for a chat about life in the great outdoors, or his kayak in particular, was fumbling with a pack of chewing gum.

Did that man ever do anything but hang out by the coffee machine?

Well, maybe Harry did look like a hard-boiled version of Bear Grylls but he was also good at talking about the spiritual aspects of life. So, I was happy to meet him there. Harry was the first one in the unit I had confided in when I converted to the Catholic Church and it was Harry who knew most about my sadder life experiences.

'You look kind of sad, Henrik,' he said.

'We were soldiers, all right but Harry knew well when to address each other by last name and when…when not to.'

It said H.M. Christensen on my uniform. In the helicopter I was called GOM – that was my flying name.

Unlike the American pilots, we were not allowed to choose our own, so there was no Goose or Maverick on the air base in Karup. Ours was determined by a guy in an office at the flight school who formed a three-letter word out of the letters in our name and made sure we were not named anything really embarrassing. 'Henrik?'

I nodded to Harry. 'Yes.' I was a little sad and then we stood there at the coffee vending machine in Karup and talked about life for most of half-an-hour.

Harry had said his goodbyes many times and he had a very calming effect on me. And after another cup of coffee I was back at the desk again. Harry taught me that it is tough but saying your goodbyes like this, in advance, is an educational experience. Everything will become clearer. It puts life into perspective and helps to make the true values in life visible.

Dearest Lisa.
My lovely wife.

Well, damn it, that was the end of it. And it was finally going so well.

I love you and the more I got to know you, with your sweet and patient being the more I cared for you. Even though I was sometimes an angry old geezer with a hysterical need for order and with very little patience.

49

I am dead but will live on in your memories. I know you will think of me and the good times we had together. Let's meet in our dreams, in an English manor garden with sunshine and "Tea House".

I am grateful to you for showing me my ability to think. I think you will eventually find another boyfriend who will be good to you. That would be great. As long as you think about me every once in a while, especially when you see yellow and orange flowers.

I love you forever and I believe we will meet again.

Sincerely, forever,
Your husband, Henrik.

4. Scramble Lynx

At my command or in self-defence, open fire.
"Scramble Lynx!"

The order reverberated through the intercom, making the loudspeakers everywhere on the ship quiver. Scramble is a bit like take-off, only it has to happen extremely fast. Our standing order was to be in the air within ten minutes, if the alarm went off. If a merchant ship was attacked. I happened to be close to the operations room and poked my head in.

'What is going on?'

The marine at the first screen looked up.

'Pirate attack. They have set the alarm off on Channel 16,' he stated laconically. I took the information in.

'Position?'

He pointed to the flashing green dot on the screen.

I received a position of the supposed pirate ship. A dhow with two skiffs in tow, it seemed. The next moment I hurried down to the helicopter deck. Along the way, I picked up my survival equipment, which, as planned, was ready on the bench in front of the dressing room and fastened it around my sand-coloured flight suit. The technician had been so kind as to get my gun out of the weapons locker and placed it by my things. It was customary for us to bring loaded handguns every time we left the ship. We had to be able to protect ourselves if the helicopter crashed and it was far from certain that we would be able to reach one of the carbine rifles stored in the back of the helicopter in case we hit the ground and had to shoot ourselves free.

The helicopter deck was already bustling with activity when I got there. Swiftly, I greeted the ship's Flight Deck Director and the crew who were already removing the lashings on the helicopter. JIR, the Gazelle and Bjarne were ready in the Lynx that gleamed majestically in the strong African sun. JIR, our pilot, had started the engine.

Bjarne was ready at the machine gun while the Gazelle prepared his sniper rifle. I gave them a nod and wiped my forehead.

My shadow was just below me, barely visible. It was insanely hot, almost unbearable. Inside the cockpit as well, even though we had had sunshields in the windows all morning.

JIR wiped a drop of sweat off the nose and gave me a thumbs up.

'Ready?'

I nodded and buckled up in to the seat next to him. Plugged in the helmet and patted my hands lightly over my vest to check that everything was as it should be.

Right side of the vest: Gun, GPS transmitter, a Velcro and plastic tourniquet, so we could perform first aid for ourselves if we were shot while sitting in the helicopter. Left side: Signal equipment, night-time distress flares and orange smoke flares for daytime. Extra ammunition for the gun. Scarf, knife and a harness cutter that could cut the seat belt, if the helicopter went down in the water.

One time, which was enough for me, I had tried being stuck under water in our training tank and had to put my hand on my helmet to signal to the divers that I needed help.

I put on my helmet. It was prepared for night vision goggles. I was not going to need that today. However, I did have my little monocular with me. It was not really an authorised part of our equipment and according to the long list of regulations in the Defence it was forbidden to carry this type of equipment because we had not received training in using it.

But frankly – a monocular?

I liked it and if there was anything you learned from working with the frogmen, it was to collect as much equipment as possible. You had a much better sense of knowing what you might need than the paper-pushers did.

Finally, I put on my bulletproof vest. It was heavy as lead. And hot as hell. For the same reason, I only used it when we were approaching a target.

'We need to find a dhow, a mother ship. I have the position,' I said.

We had been in Somalia for a couple of weeks.

Damn, it was so hot – all the time. The sweat made your clothes cling to your body and you learned to appreciate air conditioning and fresh water as some of the cornerstones of a well-functioning life. 14 days earlier we had flown from Karup to Bahrain, where Absalon was anchored and drove for an hour through the most barren area I had ever seen – a moonscape – to get to the harbour. It was heavily secured, fenced and plastered with guards. Only after getting through security and to the end of the farthest dock, we had seen the outline of the warship and the writing 'L-16' that lit up the grey hull.

It felt safe and majestic at the same time. HDMS Absalon was an impressively large ship.

We dragged our luggage up the gangway, our shirts already soaked. Fortunately, our helmets and other equipment had been sent ahead. I had two big suitcases for my own things.

We gave the guard a nod and gathered, all sweaty, at the helicopter office on the landing at the bottom of the hangar. Our blue bird stood there resting with the rotor blades folded. It looked fully equipped. Oil dripped out in just the right places and the large machine gun was mounted and folded and shone beautifully with its thin layer of oil in the red light. The departing crew told us how they had located a pirate mothership a few days earlier, how their ladders and weapons had looked and how the presumed pirates had surrendered immediately.

We could only hope that the ones we met would do the same.

The Lynx was in the air after nine minutes.

'Initial heading 120. Roger, all systems go. Brumbass out.'

The Dhow was heading for two merchant ships, we were told. It would take us about half an hour to get there, I calculated.

Shit.

I got in touch with the German surveillance aircraft, which had initially spotted the target and made the alarm call.

'I am still circling the area, 2,000 feet,' he said.

'Roger, enroute, ETA 30…no, 25 minutes – staying below 1,000 feet on QNH 1015,' I replied. JIR smiled.

It was not our first flight over the Gulf of Aden. After a few days in the port of Bahrain, Absalon had set its course towards the east of the Gulf of Aden. From there, we had taken a few training trips with the Frogman Corps in the boats below us and we had also started doing the daily surveillance trips and had gotten an impression of the shipping traffic in the area.

Which was relatively manageable, we soon discovered.

The smuggling of drugs in the Gulf of Aden went from east to west, from Pakistan to Europe. The smuggling of humans went from south to north, from Africa to the Arabian Peninsula. The smuggling of weapons went the opposite way.

The large merchant ships went east or west at high speed. From the air, you could clearly see the concentration along that same line, a ship corridor recommended to avoid pirates. The big dots clumped together on the radar. Super tankers and container ships.

But we looked for the small targets that were more difficult to detect. The small boats that could act as mother ships for pirates searching for their next prey.

When we flew, we also constantly listened to the common international shipping channel, channel 16. This was probably the place a mayday call would be heard first.

We could feel the nervousness of the merchant ships clearly when they communicated with each other.

On the second day we waved at a Maersk ship. The captain went outside and waved back. Right there you felt a little bit cool flying past them like that, low with the cabin door open and the heavy machine gun poking out.

However, some days would pass before we ended up needing it.

Twenty minutes after we had taken off from Absalon, we could see the German P3C Orion surveillance aircraft which had spotted the suspicious looking dhow.

Simultaneously, a small target began to blink on the radar. I called Absalon.

'New unknown 1001, in position…'

And soon after:

'U1001, certain Somali dhow towing two skiffs, U1001 now suspect 1001.'

Our unknown target had been transformed into a suspected pirate ship.

When we were to assess whether a ship was suspicious, there were always a number of points I went through in my head.

Tripwires, we called them.

Indications that the ship we were looking at had pirates and pirate equipment on board.

This one had both ladders and weapons placed in the two skiffs which he dragged after the dhow. Fishermen from Yemen on the other side of the Gulf of Aden, north of Somalia, often got pretty far out to sea. But it certainly was not fishermen we observed here.

The tension in the cabin rose. 'Prepare HMG,' I told Bjarne. HMG. *Heavy machinegun.*

'HMG prepared,' Bjarne replied.

Simultaneously, the Gazelle from the Frogman Corps prepared his sniper rifle.

The rest of his colleagues would soon appear in a boat below us.

*

There had been a party in the area of the mess and cafeteria when we had arrived at Absalon in Bahrain. This usually happened when the ship was in port. Someone gave me a much-needed cold beer, and with that in my hand I had greeted several old acquaintances, including a former classmate from the Defence College. He was now head of special forces, the SMTF-group, aboard Absalon.

Mr Schwann, we used to call him back then at the school, named after a pretty annoying stickler of the rules character in the Danish tv-series Matador, who he reminded us of.

He had given my hand a firm squeeze and patted me on the shoulder. Luckily, it seemed he had forgotten all times I tried to mess with him back in the day. I still struggled to forget the many bruises he had given me in return.

Mr Schwann preferred to settle things physically, but this also meant no hard feelings afterwards.

We had had a couple of drinks together, and shortly after, the helmsman from the Frogman Corps had danced energetically past me, heading for the toilet before he had filled up the bar and joined us.

Now Mr Schwann was 25 minutes behind me, back on the ship, in radio contact with the helmsman, who steered the RHIB towards the coordinates I had given him.

When the task force at the Horn of Africa started, the suspected pirates usually stopped when the NATO forces appeared and flexed their muscles. This time was an exception. The dhow zigzagged at full speed beneath us, apparently indifferent to the large machine gun pointing at him. When the frogmen arrived shortly after, he tried sailing into them.

'Now there's someone who's been chewing too much khat,' JIR said. There was hardly any doubt about that. Most Somali pirates chewed daily on the euphoric, green leaves that grow all over in most of East Africa and offer an easy and inexpensive escape from everyday hardships.

The very next moment we saw the first black figures emerging from the steering house on the dhow. They were armed with the usual AK47 rifles and an RPG.

RPG. Rocket-propelled grenade. A rocket launcher.

AK-47. A cheap, but functional Russian storm rifle invented by Mikhail Kalashnikov in 1947 and for years the preferred weapon among terrorists, rebels and communist soldiers. And now pirates.

'Load HMG, the goal is the dhow, on my command or in self-defence open fire,' I said to Bjarne.

It was like a dance between the frogmen, the pirates and us. Continuously, we placed ourselves in new positions. As pilot, JIR's biggest challenge was to maintain the cooling of the air through the turbine engines of the Lynx which was already struggling to deliver in the hot and humid air as it was.

Then the frogmen below us fired the first warning shots, and seconds later the helmsman called me on the radio from the boat.

'Shoot in front of them, repeat, shoot in front of them!' he exclaimed hectically.

As the first thing, according to international procedure, we had to throw orange smoke down in front of the Somali ship as a sign that they should stop. But there was no time for that now. It was dissatisfying for the frogmen that the pirates apparently were controlling the course of action, and they were nervous about what they might do.

I turned around and gave Bjarne a nod. "Open fire."

There are procedures for everything in the Armed Force, and when it comes to international missions, the rule book does not get smaller. We had gone through our rules of engagement, or just ROEs, over and over before we left. And we kept going over them during trips because NATO constantly changed the rules for what we were allowed to do. Every time we were on our way to attack a new ship, we had to be briefed first by a military lawyer.

Initially, we basically did not have permission to sail into or fly over another country's territorial waters. That was typically 12 nautical miles, 22 kilometres, from the coast. Rather quickly, it was changed so that we had permission to go all the way to the coast but not further than that.

We had to "keep our feet wet", as it was called.

On the other hand, we were initially allowed to fly very close to the supposed pirate ships. This rule was changed later, because someone thought that waving the machine gun just above the heads of the pirates could annoy them unnecessarily.

I quickly gave up on finding out why and how the different rules came about. Knowing who really decided what was impenetrable. We were associated with a NATO force, but most ROEs were agreed upon at UN level. Some rules were also agreed upon in direct cooperation with the NATO-friendly Somali government which at one time gained control of the northern part of the country's coast. Finally, any country was free to go into so-called national mode. This meant that, for a while, a country withdrew from the NATO coalition and instead acted on their own. Something which especially the Americans took advantage of, if a US ship was hijacked and they needed to use more power than the UN and NATO mandates allowed.

It was easy to be a little envious of this type of determination, especially considering that the Danish frogmen were probably even better warriors than the otherwise famous American Navy Seals, who were also stationed in the Gulf of Aden.

There were also rules that said how close the pirates had to be in attacking a ship, before we were allowed to shoot at them. In the beginning, we were only allowed to shoot at people, if they had crawled aboard a ship. Later, we were allowed to shoot, if they were going up a ladder. But always only at the body, not the head. Unless they pointed a weapon at us. That rule was non-negotiable.

If our lives were in danger, we had to defend ourselves.

In fact, that day in the Gulf of Aden, one of the Somalis lifted his RPG and aimed at us, and I know the Gazelle had him in his sight, ready to kill. But it did not become necessary to shoot, because a split second later, all the pirates ducked when Bjarne's machine gun planted the first row of projectiles in the water right in front of the dhow. When that did not stop the boat and the Somalis did not throw their weapons, he dropped the next round in the bow of their ship and with a pleased expression on his face, he then severed the two skiffs the pirates had on tow.

The two shattered skiffs lay low in the water and hampered the speed of the dhow, so the pirates cut them free and let them sink.

Thus, they could not perform an effective attack on a merchant ship, thus they no longer posed any danger to any civilians and thus our role was also exhausted.

The pirates would undoubtedly sail to the coast and get hold of two new attack boats, but our ROEs did not allow us to do more. The frogmen's boat was already on its way back to Absalon, while we, while keeping a safe distance, flew over the pacified pirates, so the Gazelle could photograph the result of our work. In addition to being a sharpshooter, it was also his task to document what we were doing. So, throughout the trip, he had taken pictures whenever possible.

It was only when we returned to Absalon and looked through the pictures that it became clear to us how close our first task in Somalia had also been of being our last. When you zoomed in, one of the pictures clearly showed two of the pirates shooting directly at us.

5. HDMS Absalon

Britta Maersk, this is the Danish naval helicopter 134.
Help is on its way.

I have always loved sailing on large ships.

A large ship is like a mobile community on the sea. You have what you need to meet most needs. A bunk, a mess room where you eat.

Toilet and bath.

There are different kinds of people to talk to all over but the size of the ship also makes it possible to be alone for a while. To look at the sea while thinking about the big and small things in life.

I often did that.

A ship like HDMS Absalon is an organism, it is alive and often in motion.

The organism is powered by its heart – the machine in the bottom of the vessel, the one who faithfully delivers momentum and life in the form of power to the nerves of the ship. There is always machine crew on duty in the machine's control room, always activity on the ship.

The operations room, the Ops-room, is the brain of the organism. Up here, the ship's thinking takes place and from here operations are controlled. Here, the sensory input of the organism is monitored and processed.

In the Ops-room, there are constantly battle information crew operating the ship's sensors and communication. All managed by a tactical duty officer. When all is calm, the brain follows the basic routine. But when an operation is in progress, the brain is in full swing. Then the Commanding Officer and the second in command are also in the Ops-room with their various experts and contacts from the special forces right next to them.

As soon as you pass the blue curtain into the Ops-room, you can feel the concentrated suspense in the room.

The head of the organism is the bridge from where the navigator skilfully manoeuvres the large ship through the water. All the while keeping in contact with the Ops-room.

The organs in the ship are many and count the galley with chefs and bakers, ship offices with administration crew, a small hospital with a doctor and nurses, a mobile church with a naval priest, electrical and electronics workshop, a weapons workshop and lawyers, interpreters, language officers and intelligence staff from all three forces.

We were all kinds of people there.

When it is offshore, there are about 100 men and women who are permanently manning a ship like Absalon. There, they are all marines. Even the ones who cook or clean toilets.

The baker bakes bread daily and the electrician installs sockets. But they are also both, like the rest of the crew, professional soldiers who can grab a weapon if needed. On a warship, everyone must be soldiers, because everyone has a dual function. At Least. Several have three or four functions. A daily routine and a number of alternative roles in special situations. For example, if the helicopter gets into trouble and needs to perform an emergency landing on the ship, it may be the guy who rinses dishes in the washing-up unit who is ready at the front of the deck as a fireman. We had a large chart that showed everyone's different functions, and everyone also had a card on them listing their functions, so that they could remember their own tasks in the different situations.

Rolls, we call it.

For example, if we run the "ready ship" roll, it means that the ship is in danger. Then it will suddenly be announced on the intercom that we have that roll, and then people change function. Then, the guy who rinses plates in they galley's washing-up unit may have to go up and pass grenades to the one who loads the cannon.

My rolls were pretty easy to remember. If the ship was sinking and we switched to the salvage roll, then just like the rest of the crew, I had to position myself by the life raft I belonged to. In other rolls, I just had to report to the helicopter office. If nothing else, so people knew where I was, if the Lynx needed to be sent out.

Who then decides what actually happens on such a ship? Well, the head of Absalon was our Commander senior grade, Frank Trojahn. The Commander senior grades rank corresponds to lieutenant-colonel in the army. He does the overall thinking and steering of the ship. He's the boss. It is he who determines the course and when to attack or hold back. Of course, while taking into consideration some limitations given by the international authorities and the politicians back home in Denmark. Therefore, Trojahn was always in close contact with the Naval Commanding Officer at Holmen in Copenhagen, when dangerous situations arose.

It was not always possible tell what good ideas the elected officials had enforced upon him.

Second in command on Absalon was the Commander. That rank corresponds to Major on land. While the Commander senior grade controlled the ship outwardly, the Commander controlled the troops internally.

The hotel boss, we also just called him.

My closest superior was the pilot of the helicopter. Someone must have the final say when you are hanging in five tons of steel several hundred metres above the sea, and there can never be any doubt about the hierarchy.

In reality, however, the people in the ship's operations room were the ones who had the overview, when we were on a mission, and therefore decided what was going to happen.

On the ship, people often kept to their own kind. Like in other big workplaces. We also ate in different mess rooms, which strengthened this behaviour. The privates sat in the cafeteria, the sergeants in the sergeants' mess room and we, the officers, sat in the officers' mess room. It was a relic of the past to divide people that way on ships. And it was quite sensible because this way you could talk about others behind their backs or talk about work without the wrong ones hearing it. Nevertheless, the food was the same for all, prepared by the same cook. Actually, it was probably a little better in the sergeants' mess room, as the head of the galley himself was sergeant.

The kitchen on a ship like this, the galley, is one of the most important organs because without food and drink the heroes do not function and if you want to take the Danish Navy out of the game, you just have to make sure that hundreds of marines get diarrhoea at the same time. For this very reason, our doctor who was responsible for the hygiene on board ensured that one of the nurses checked the kitchen facilities weekly.

The various cafeterias and mess rooms on the ship were located on the main deck. The coffee machines were also placed here and this was the place you hung out if you needed some small talk. The engine room and the control room, from which the machines were controlled, were situated under the main deck. As was our flexible deck where we could park large vehicles or set up a field hospital in emergency situations or, as became the case later, prison cells.

The privates also had their quarters under the main deck. The lower the rank you had, the further down in the ship you lived. The ones at the bottom of the hierarchy lived in four-bunk rooms, each bunk with its own small closet with a shared shower, far down in Absalon's stomach. The commander senior grade lived in an apartment at the top of the ship, complete with office and living room, where he could hold meetings in a homely environment. He could even have his meals served up there if that was what he wanted.

In the middle, just above the main deck, the sergeants and officers lived. And also, myself. I stayed in a two-bunk room with room for a small desk, a small private bathroom and a closet for each of the lodgers with room enough for our flight equipment. On my first trips to the Horn of Africa, I lived with our pilot, MER. A round-headed, thin-haired guy, slightly older than me. MER was from the western part of Copenhagen and came from a real working-class family. He was a tough guy, but not so tough that you couldn't soften him with alcohol.

'You are my best friend. My best friend,' he used to say all the time, when we were in port and had had some drinks.

A quarter of the crew on Absalon were women.

The women lived together, but also by rank. So, if you were lucky to be the only female officer, you got your own cabin on the ship.

Lukaf, that's what we called our small cabins.

A lot can happen when people are stuck together on a ship for the three months each mission lasted. And having both sexes on board the ship did not make it any easier. It was not like anyone were obvious about it by practically holding hands in the mess room or anything and I also don't think that had been tolerated. But there was no doubt that several people made a romantic connection during such a posting. Of course, it could result in terrible drama, especially if people then split up again but I never experienced problems with that. There was just one thing to remember that if you flirted with someone, preferably they had to have the same rank as yourself.

If you flirted with someone of a higher rank than your own, you could quickly become a laughing stock. If you flirted with someone of a lower rank, you could quickly get a sexual harassment case filed against you. Theoretically, that is. Not that I know anything about any of these things.

As a helicopter crew, we basically had two kinds of tasks on Absalon. One was emergency aid for ships that were being or had been hijacked. No matter where it or its crew came from. The ships were either spotted by us, by one of the NATO forces' surveillance aircrafts, as was the case with my first meeting with the pirates or had made an alarm call, either by contacting someone in their home country or by making an alarm call on the international shipping frequency. Most pirate attacks were discovered because a merchant ship had heard a mayday on the international sea frequency, channel 16 and passed on the message.

The second kind of task, which was more peaceful and which we fortunately did most of the time was to monitor the waters off Somalia. It was our everyday routine. A normal day was typically like this:

We got up at six o'clock, took a bath, got some breakfast in the mess or at the helicopter office, and then got a briefing from the duty officer in the Ops-room about the activities for the day. If it appeared that the day would be normal, we got ready for the first flight of the day while the rest of the ship was awakened over the intercom by an assisting officer who was always a bit too perky.

'Good morning, Absalon. Time to get out of the bunks, it's 7 am.'

It wasn't like we didn't want to sleep an hour extra ourselves. But statistics showed that most pirate attacks took place early in the morning at dusk. Probably because the Somalis would rather lie in the shade and chew khat once the sun started baking over the Horn of Africa.

So, when the pirates got up, we did too.

We had a fixed "box" we searched every morning – a space on the map, calculated down to the decimals of the coordinates which we had agreed upon with the rest of the NATO force. Another helicopter from another ship searched the box next to it and so on. There we flew while rubbing the sleep from our eyes while we both watched the ships that looked like targets, typically those lying low in the water sailing slowly, and with possible pirates. Especially in the beginning we could clearly hear the merchant ships' nervousness on the common radio channel when they were talking about the suspicious, fast-moving wooden boats they had spotted. Then we had to take a closer look for them and for the most part, happily reassure them that they had only observed some Yemeni fishermen hunting dolphins.

Later, our routine flights over the sea were replaced by more and more flights along the Somali coast, where we looked for pirate camps. Meanwhile, our frogman took pictures that we passed on to the intelligence service who was keeping an eye on how the number of pirates and pirate fleets evolved.

It was strange to leave a high-tech ship like Absalon, with all its flashing screens and conveniences to be hovering, only 20 minutes later, over a village that looked like something from the Iron Age, filled with goats and dromedaries and with some pieces of orange plastic as the primary defence against wind and weather.

We typically landed on Absalon again at half past eight. An hour and a half like that in a helicopter corresponded to half a day's work because you were fully concentrated all the way.

Then you needed to rest for a while and fill up with both coffee and water again. During the afternoon, there was typically some administrative work to be done, some paper that had to be moved from one box to another, as we said before we left for yet another flight for an hour and a half while the sun slowly went down. When we came back, we ate and then the rest of the evening was spent playing cards, reading or watching TV. Either in the common rooms or in our cabin.

If the day had been sufficiently tough, you could curse and complain about the bad network connection which made it a painful experience to get through the choppy broadcast of the Danish news that we were able to watch with a 24-hour delay. Actually, it was technically possible to get enough power on the Internet so that we would almost be able to watch live TV from Denmark but most of the bandwidth was reserved for the satellite communication of the Ops-room, so, in this particular area, we had to live with the feeling of being set back to a more primitive time.

When we were off duty, I usually spent the time with the others from the Lynx crew or the frogmen. We had a warm friendship with the guys from the Frogman Corps, especially because we were dependent on each other during operations.

On the one hand, we gave the frogs protection from the air so that they could perform their tasks under more secure conditions. Top cover, as it is called. You could hear the gratitude in the voice of the helmsman over the radio when we, in the darkness, followed the planned procedures and came to their assistance if they were pressured by a superior opponent. You could see their satisfaction when they passed the helicopter in the hangar and with a casual look controlled that the heavy machine gun was in its right position and looked well maintained.

On the other hand, we were, to say the least, also happy that the frogs were along for the mission. Today, as the sound of lapping salt water waves and the dust have settled, and the Horn of Africa is nothing but a memory, I often still miss the pleasant conversations with Gazelle and Pas and the many talks I had with Gartner over coffee. They were nice guys, but they were also the ones who had to risk their lives to save us, if we fell into the water or went down behind enemy lines.

Of course, the co-operation and friendship got even closer due to the fact that we had one of their sharp shooters in the helicopter and by the fact that the frogmen were on the helicopter deck constantly because it was the best place to work on your tan or exercise when the heat allowed it. The frogmen were also quite keen on training fast-roping when the time allowed it and when they could talk us into it.

We needed this, when, shortly after our first encounter with the enemy, our assistance was needed again.

*

The date was November 2, 2008, and it was around noon in the middle of the worst heat when the alarm went off.

Two small, fast motorboats, skiffs, were heading directly towards the Danish tanker Britta Maersk which was located in the waters between Somalia and Yemen.

The ship was on its way from Singapore with vegetable oil in the tanks and was headed to Jeddah in Saudi Arabia to refuel.

'Scramble Lynx!'

When the roll sounded over the intercom, the pirates were already shooting at the tanker.

Damn it.

We had been given the alarm too late and were too far away to prevent the attack. Fortunately, most ships, at least the Danish ones had at that time initiated and practiced a number of security procedures in case of pirate attacks. The crew on Britta Maersk did everything just by the book: They locked the superstructure on the ship and activated the ship's fire extinguishing system, so that water was sprayed over the side of the ship. It could possibly win them some time until help arrived. Then they locked themselves in a room below deck.

Five of the frogmen jumped aboard the helicopter which lifted off the deck six minutes after the alarm went off.

When we arrived a few minutes later, we couldn't detect any pirates on the ship.

Everything seemed quiet.

'Where the hell are their boats?' Some were shaking their heads. I called on channel 16–156.8 MHz.

'Britta Maersk, this is Danish naval helicopter 134.' The radio made a scratchy sound.

'Here is Britta Maersk.'

You could hear the joy in the captain's voice, not least because he was spoken to in Danish. Unfortunately, he couldn't help us clear up where the pirates who had shot at his ship just a moment ago had gone. He sat with the crew in the locked, bulletproof room below deck. From here, he could control the ship and keep in radio contact with the outside world but he had no opportunity of seeing what was happening on his ship.

'Keep going on a steady course and steady speed and we will come and drop some people off to search the ship,' I announced over the radio.

JIR put the Lynx in position over the tanker and 20 seconds later, five frogmen were heading down the ropes towards the deck. The tension in the air was so thick you could cut it with a knife because no one knew if the pirates were ready on the deck and were going to shoot at them.

But there was no one shooting at us in the Arabian Sea that day.

I changed frequency to a more private line and reported to the captain that we had put elite forces on board and that he just had to stay calm.

There were bullet holes in the walls of Britta Maersk but no pirates.

It took three to four hours for the armed frogmen to finish searching the ship. During the search, one of the RHIB boats came in support and helped. Only then did the people on board Absalon tell the captain that the crew could lock themselves back out.

It was always very nice to read the Danish news in the evening after an operation. The Defence rarely told the media everything we did. But an operation like the one with Britta Maersk was good PR for our efforts. And, at the same time, it was a good way to tell our family and friends what we were doing and working with down here.

'Pirates attack Danish tanker,' our national newspaper Politiken wrote on their website that same evening.

We felt a little proud of the press's report on our actions. It felt good knowing that people at home in Denmark got some insight into our very different everyday life down here in the heat. Even though we were able to Skype with our families back home, when the internet connection allowed it, we still were not allowed to talk about what we were doing and where we were. It was in our own best interests not to compromise operational safety, nor were we permitted to write about our experiences on Facebook. We could not risk giving the enemy information about ourselves so he could take his counter-measures.

The pirates were also on Facebook.

They even read Danish newspapers' websites, we were later to find out.

6. Helicopter in Distress

Pan-pan, pan-pan, pan-pan, Brumbass with single engine failure, approaching from the east.

Lynx is the English name of a wild animal in the cat family. And our beloved helicopter was indeed also bought in England. Denmark has had Lynx helicopters since the early 80s, and we owned eight when we had the most. Today, we have seven because one crashed in Greenland after getting a defect on the tail. However, no one was hurt. All the Danish Lynx helicopters have, since we bought them, had their structural frames reinforced, so they are durable enough to land on a ship, and have been equipped with a so-called harpoon that can latch on to the landing grid so they are capable of landing on a ship.

If you follow the procedures, there is room for six soldiers in such a helicopter, plus two of us up front who control it. In Africa, we were four in total – a pilot, a tactical coordinator, a technician and a sniper from the Frogman Corps. There were two technicians on Absalon at a time but the pilot and I were the only ones with our functions on the ship.

If one of us got sick, we would not fly out that day. For the same reason, we were never sick. It was the same with the helicopter, we only had one with us, so if it broke and the technicians could not repair it, then we would not be flying anymore on that trip. Fortunately, that never happened.

The Lynx helicopter has two turbine engines that make the rotor turn. The two engines each provide about 1200 horsepower under normal weather conditions. Down by Somalia, it is hot and humid and the two 1200 hp engines quickly weaken. In reality, this meant that we were pressured if we got an engine failure on one engine. If that happened, we would no longer be able to stay in a hover on the port side of the ship just before landing. Therefore, we were constantly aware of engine temperature and oil pressure during our flights.

One day, warm as always, we were returning to the ship after a monitoring task. I drank the last of my water and once again checked mother's position on the TDS.

We always called Absalon "mother".

'KUB, we will be there in 20 minutes, I am checking in on the landing frequency and then you will get it.'

KUB turned his face to look at me. He was one of our most experienced pilots.

'Fine with me, Gommi. I have to take a leak.'

Relieving yourself was generally a bit of a challenge. We drank lots of fluids in the heat, but if you couldn't hold it in, you had to pee in the suit. There were not many who wanted to do that unless it was absolutely necessary. Luckily, we were rarely in the air more than one and a half hours at a time, but just as brilliant KUB was at flying a helicopter, just as terrible he was at planning his visits to the toilet.

His eyes scanned the engine instruments.

'What the heck, I think the engine temperature in engine 2 is fluctuating?'

We all looked at the pointer which now rose sharply, while the pointer in the oil pressure above it just dropped.

In my head, I quickly went through the list of steps I knew from several hours in the simulator.

Maintain aircraft control. Analyse situation.

Take proper action.

We were all very calm. We had completed the exercise with a dead engine before and besides, we would almost be able to fly down and land on KUB's ego alone.

But nevertheless, none of us wanted to get our feet wet and especially not on a Somali beach after an emergency landing.

'We will shut down engine 2 and make a pan call,' KUB said with a loud, but calm voice.

A pan call was the step just before mayday and always began with the words *pan-pan, pan-pan, pan-pan.*

'Get checklist and point to ECL 2.'

I pointed to the right engine condition lever. A kind of throttle for engine 2. 'Confirmed,' KUB said.

'Pull it back.'

Then red and orange lamps starting lighting up on the CWP, central warning panel and we heard the warning siren in our headset in the helmet. It was expected and we continued with the checklist.

'On failed engine, ECL HP cock off, LP cock shut, X-feed open, busbar coupling select manual, land as soon as practicable and single engine landing carry out.'

It was in 2010 that the one engine failed, just as KUB had to pee. I was on my third trip to the Horn of Africa and was gradually becoming an experienced pirate hunter.

I had been off for 44 days in 2008 and coming home to Denmark after the baptism of fire had been nice.

Lisa had gotten a job as a psychologist in Norway and I enjoyed my time alone in our big apartment in Tolbodgade in Copenhagen, so I could be close to my girls. It was nice to get away from Africa. Occasionally I rented a car, so I could pick up Sofie and Laura in Lyngby and then we went on a picnic in Kongens Have, the King's Garden with Rosenborg as a marvellous background.

The apartment was also right next to Nyhavn, that bustling part of inner Copenhagen and I hung out there a lot when I was not with the girls. I even became a regular in the Scottish pub on the corner.

'Hi, Henrik,' they said when I stepped inside. I also got a discount.

I should probably have seen that as a kind of warning. But there are no lights that blink when there is something wrong with the human engine.

In 2009, I had gone to Africa again. Same ship, same helicopter, new crew.

I had updated my last will and caught myself changing the names of some of the ones I wanted to carry the coffin, if I died during my posting. Stubbornness, I suppose. We did not find any pirates on my trip in 2009. We mainly met a lot of fishermen from Yemen and sometimes vessels that smuggled people from Somalia to Yemen, where they would try to start a new life on the bottom of society. We let them pass.

The most exciting event was actually a trip with some French colleagues.

We had been docked in Djibouti, and I had arranged a flight with a French Breguet Atlantique, a naval patrol aircraft that was stationed on a US air base. We flew on a six-hour surveillance in the Gulf of Aden with "Resistance 71" as their nickname was. That aircraft was considerably faster than the helicopter and covered almost the entire bay on a single trip. Back in the cabin, their French TACCO sat with helpers on each side. I didn't have helpers. There were loads of screens and equipment in the French aircraft and a well-stocked fridge.

In the tail section there were parachutes hanging near the hatch we were to exit from if problems occurred in the air. When I stuck my head into one of the glass domes in the sides of the plane, I could see the tail from outside. It was pretty trippy. Back at the TACCO, I could see how the French had mapped out the shipping traffic and when they found something suspicious, a crew member walked into the cockpit and crawled down a ladder between the pilot's legs to end up in the plane's glass nose from which it was possible to take pictures. It was pretty cool.

Instead of disembarking in Bahrain and flying home, I sailed to Europe in 2009. Absalon was also going home.

We left the Gulf of Aden through the Bab el-Mandeb strait between Yemen and Ethiopia, headed north through the Red Sea, up towards the Suez Canal. Sailing through the Suez Canal was a huge experience. You could see land on both sides, and there was a close traffic of merchant ships, which constantly passed us in the opposite direction on the way from the Mediterranean and down towards the Gulf of Aden. In front of us, ships sailing the same way as Absalon sailed towards the Mediterranean – the motorway of the sea. I celebrated my birthday in Alexandria on the Mediterranean coast of Egypt, where one of the seven wonders of the world had stood, the great lighthouse from the time just after Alexander the Great. Here, the world's largest library had been, at the time of Cleopatra and Julius Caesar. A couple of days later, our helicopter group got off in Catania on the east side of Sicily, while Absalon returned to a great reception in Copenhagen.

It was much harder coming home the second time. Lisa was back from Norway, and I saw errors everywhere. It was normal, said the psychologist. But still, I missed being alone, I probably missed being able to spend more time at the pub but most of all, I missed the action. I had sweet dreams about the day we had shot the pirate's skiffs in two and the day we had put down the frogmen on Britta Maersk. And I was honestly relieved when I was told that I was going on my third trip. Away from the everyday grind of couple-life to fill out the role I had come to love. The role of pirate hunter.

We were basically in safe surroundings that day in 2010 when we hung over the dark African sea with only one functional engine. We were in a known situation, not least from our training in the Lynx simulator in the Netherlands and Germany.

But it was still nerve-racking.

Having to report "helicopter in distress" is not fun.

'Blue Lynx down,' I caught myself mumbling. It would be a bad title for a movie. I continued with a call on the radio to the ship.

'Pan-pan, pan-pan, pan-pan, Brumbass with single engine failure on number two, approaching from the east, 400 feet, speed 1 double 0, ETA 15 minutes, request single engine running landing upon arrival.'

Yes, we had baptised our helicopter Brumbass like bumblebee in Danish.

The ship's helicopter controlling officer, HCO for short, responded immediately. 'Roger, your pan call is acknowledged, pigeons to mother 260/25 nautical miles – any other signs of failure?'

'Negative.'

We flipped one page further in the checklist for single engine landing and reached the point where we had to lighten the helicopter as much as possible.

We looked kiddingly at the sniper from the Frogman Corps, before we just settled with dumping some fuel.

I calculated the landing speed with the now lighter helicopter and we did a pre-landing check. The ship was in sight, it came at full speed towards us, and, on the starboard-side, you could see a rubber boat crew waiting to help us, if we were to fall into the water.

If anyone should happen to be in doubt about it, flying a helicopter is quite difficult. They say it is the most difficult thing to do right after heart surgery but I don't know if that is true. I don't know about heart surgery but I have, however, tried to fly a helicopter. As TACCO, it was not my primary focus but of course I had learned the necessary things. When the helicopter is going fast, it is easy to control. But when you slow down, it gets difficult. Then everything must be coordinated – heeling, balance, height. Keeping the helicopter in the air when it is not accelerating is like balancing an egg.

The pilot has a control stick between his legs, it's also called a cyclic stick. He typically controls it with his right hand and with it, he can change the flight direction – forward, backward, sideways, all 360 degrees around. By his left hand he has another control stick, also called a collective stick. With that, he can change the angle of all the helicopter rotor blades at the same time. To put it simply, it controls whether the helicopter is flying up or down.

The angle of the tail rotor is controlled by two pedals. It is used to compensate for the torque of the main rotor as it is called in aviation lingo. In normal terms, this means that the helicopter will crash into the sea if the tail rotor does not help to balance it.

If one of the helicopter's two engines fails, landing becomes difficult. There is not enough power to hover – to stand still in the air. This is why you always attempt doing a so-called rolling landing on an aircraft carrier where the ship sails at full speed towards the wind, while the pilot lands. The extra headwind makes it easier for him to control the now unstable helicopter.

In addition to flying lessons, we also trained in a Lynx simulator in the Netherlands twice a year. There, we only trained the things that could go wrong. And if an accident happened, the basic principles were always the same:

Maintain aircraft control – be sure to keep the helicopter in the air. Analyse situation – analyse the situation without panicking.

Take proper action – do what gives you the best probability of getting down safely.

On film, a helicopter always goes down spinning when it crashes and in reality it is also a very good example of one of the worst things you can face: That the tail rotor breaks. It is the thing that keeps the helicopter stable. When it only concerns one engine, as it did in 2010, the problem is actually smaller. Theoretically, you can land a helicopter completely without engine power. You just have to lower it calmly so that air comes up through the rotor blades. Then you can even still steer it.

For obvious reasons, it is not possible to catapult yourself out from a helicopter like you can from a plane. If anything goes wrong, our only chance of rescue is to land it. As we often flew over water, our seat was therefore basically a collapsible inflatable boat. It would come with us, if we crawled out and would inflate when we pulled a little string.

A helicopter sinks very quickly, and should we not succeed in getting out before, we had also trained getting out under water. It took place in a swimming pool in Esbjerg, and we were blindfolded. There, we sat in a copy of a helicopter that was slowly hoisted into the water, then turned around, so you didn't know what was up and down.

Fortunately, we didn't need any of that training that day in 2010.

When we had given our pan call, hectic activity had erupted on board Esbern Snare, our ship.

'On your posts for helicopter in distress, on your posts for helicopter in distress,' they yelled on the intercom.

The lashing crew and the Flight Deck Director prepared the deck, where firefighters were also getting their equipment ready. The doctor and nurses prepared the infirmary to receive anyone wounded. Soon, another call sounded on the intercom: 'Brumbass had faults in engine 2 and will perform a rolling landing using only engine 1.'

In the helicopter, it was quieter and more peaceful. We did not have enough power in the remaining engine to land normally, so we were set up for a rolling landing along the deck, from the rear starboard corner to the front port side corner. We passed the ship and saw it turning to the port side on a more northerly course, still at full speed in order to give us a good and powerful, relative wind from the port side and onwards. We turned around and approached the ship from behind on the starboard side.

On the radio, the ship informed us:

'You are cleared to land, relative wind red 40/28 knots and flight deck is empty, but we are ready inside.'

The helicopter deck was completely empty but I could see that the commander had positioned himself behind the window of the Flight Deck Officer's small cabin.

'Wheels locks out, check harness before landing check still good,' I said in cockpit.

KUB graciously flew us across the deck, we landed and rolled a little bit and then stood still a good distance away from the hangar gate, which towered above us. Then the hatches on the side of the hangar opened, and the firefighters in their smoke diving equipment appeared, dragging on fire hoses ready to deliver water. It didn't become not necessary. We closed Brumbass down.

KUB smiled.

'Well, by the way, I still have to piss.'

7. Men Below Deck

This is Japanese Navy Fauuu Wauuu.

During 2010 we docked at the Seychelles.

The ships in the NATO force took turns docking, so there was always someone to handle the tasks in the bay. It was, however, still a possibility that we would be scrambled, meaning that we would be pulled from our hammocks and sent into the air if a Danish ship came in distress.

It was my fourth trip as a pirate hunter. This time it was Absalon's sister ship, HDMS Esbern Snare. That was my home for three warm months.

The Seychelles is an archipelago close to the Equator in the Indian Ocean. It strikes you as a tropical paradise, the first time you experience the place. The coast is like something straight out of *Robinson Crusoe* with warm, clear blue water on one side and chalk-white beaches and palms on the other.

On the main island Mahé's northeast side lies the capital, Port Victoria. The name testifies that the island has been an English colony. The fact that the more than 90,000 inhabitants now speak French tells you that the Seychelles have also been under the rule of France. The main income for the country is exports of vanilla, coconut and coconut oil, as well as tourism, including visits from cruise ships. Therefore, our grey ships were also very welcome in the Seychelles – pirates were bad for business.

Lisa travelled the long way to the archipelago and we met at a beach hotel a couple of hours after the ship's ropes had been fastened to the dock. It was amazing to sit at a beach bar with a cold beer and look at Lisa, who washed off the travel dust with a dip in the cool water. I felt a bit like James Bond.

Later, there was also time for a short safari in Kenya during a harbour docking in Mombasa. We visited the rather large Tsavo National Park. It was pure Karen Blixen country. If you paid them a fee, the Maasai would do their jumping dance and we also saw giraffes and elephants.

Esbern Snare docked every 20 days. To get supplies on board to refuel and so that we had some time to relax.

Occasionally, we docked on the African side of the Gulf of Aden. I was on a safari with my colleague, the pilot MER, when we were docked in Mombasa in Kenya for four days. But, in Africa, we usually stayed on the ship. When we docked in the harbour of the Arabian Peninsula, however, we went to land as real sailors, for instance in Muscat in Oman. We often went to a beach bar. Then half of the ship's crew lay there in swimsuits with drinks in their hands.

We were allowed to drink alcohol, the days we were in port but it seldom gave rise to trouble. That is something which happened more in the past. When Denmark had submarines, there were often problems with the crew who apparently had to blow off steam when they came out of their captivity in the cigar tube. The Danish submarine crews have smashed many a hotel around the world, it is said.

But since the submarines were phased out after the Cold War, I have not heard of anyone who needed to be picked up in the slammer by the Commander.

When we weren't having a party, went on a safari or went swimming, we could also use the time in port to find a shopping mall or a Starbucks where we could get better coffee than the mud they served on board. Sometimes we also just on stayed on the ship and relaxed. It was good to have some days where we could think of something else than pirates.

I also think it was during a trip in port when we first came up with the idea of painting skulls on the helicopter. One for every pirate ship we had stopped. If the skull had green eyes, we had taken the ship by night – the green symbolised the colour of the light we saw the world in when we were wearing our night vision goggles, our night glasses.

If the skull had a red eye, we had shot at the pirates. If both eyes were red, it meant we had killed someone.

One day in November, 2010, shortly after we had been in port, MER, Bjarne, Pas and I were scrambled. A Japanese surveillance aircraft had spotted a skiff with seven suspected pirates near us in the Gulf of Aden. There were trading ships in the area, so we had to hurry. We were in the air after eight minutes and got radio contact with the Japanese Orion aircraft. He answered.

'Brumbass, this is Japanese Navy Fauuu Wauuu, over.'

I looked at MER who also didn't understand his call sign. I asked him to repeat.

'Brumbass, this is Japanese Navy Fauuu Wauuu, over.'

We could hardly keep our composure in the cockpit and giggled loudly. I called him again.

'Japanese Navy Fauuu Wauuu, this is Brumbass, we have you and skiff in sight and we stay below 500 feet.'

We now got the real call sign of the Japanese from our ship. 'Japanese Navy 41,' someone from the Ops-room said with a sigh. We laughed a lot about that and then continued the hunt.

Bjarne was ready with the HMG. 'Same procedure as last year.' Pas caressed his sniper rifle.

That same evening, the Defence wrote on its website:

'Today, the command ship Esbern Snare has disarmed seven suspected pirates in the Gulf of Aden. The suspected pirates only surrendered after use of warning shots.

'On a patrol in the Gulf of Aden, Esbern Snare today received a message from a Japanese patrol aircraft that had observed a ship with suspected pirates only 30 miles from Esbern Snare.

'Esbern Snare's helicopter went into the air and tried to stop the vessel using warning shots in front of the vessel. The initial warning shots in front of the vessel did not cause the vessel to stop. Because the vessel posed a possible threat to the trade ships in the area, Esbern Snare switched to firing warning shots in the bow of the vessel to bring this to a halt. Two warning shots in the bow stopped the vessel.

'While Esbern Snare's helicopter hung over the floating vessel and awaited the arrival of Esbern Snare's boarding crew, the helicopter observed the suspected pirates emptying the vessel of pirate-like objects, such as ladders, grenade launchers, and a grenade.

'After the arrival of the boarding crew, the suspected pirates were detained and transferred to Esbern Snare for registration. Esbern Snare cannot prove that the suspected pirates have made an attack on a merchant ship, so the suspected pirates have been put back in their vessel with the necessary supplies to reach the coast of Somalia.'

The ships we detained, we most often blew to pieces. Two of the frogmen on board specialised in explosives and it was both an exercise and a festive occasion for them when they were allowed to transform a skiff like that into kindling wood.

Most times, our entire crew would be watching and clapping while this happened.

On other occasions, the frogmen used the ship for target practice before we got rid of it. Then they lay on the deck and pierced the pirate ship with projectiles, for the amusement of themselves and everyone else.

It was different with the pirates we caught.

Most pirates in Somalia were between 20 and 30 years old and some were down to 15. All were men. Or big boys, if you like. The UN estimated that there were about 1,500 active pirates in Somalia in those years.

Of course, the Somali men became pirates because they wanted to make money. A risky but quick way out of life in the poor cities and from a future at the bottom of an already fairly dysfunctional society. They had no higher goal with their ravaging, like the most saved types claimed at times. Well, when you interrogated them, it most often turned out that the younger pirates in particular did not know about overfishing or unfair international trade agreements. They dreamed of houses, cars, electronics and women.

In that sense, they were like most other men around the world.

Most of the Somali pirates had never worked with fishing, as the stories originally said. They were really more like

90

seekers of fortune who had come to the coast from the larger cities. As the years went by, more and more people joined, many with backgrounds as mercenaries in the various militias who fought for power in the country. And this was probably also the reason why piracy became more and more violent over time.

We knew the background and motivation of the Somalis, because we questioned the many prisoners which we took more and more of.

Actually, I don't think anyone had foreseen that we would also be acting as prison guards on board Absalon and Esbern Snare. In any event, the carpenter on the ship suddenly got busy building wooden cages when the Commanding Officers realised that not all pirates either fled or died trying. So, the carpenter looked all over the ship to find what he could use when the first interim cages on the flex deck were to be cobbled together.

Detained, suspected pirates, we called the men in the basement. We were not allowed to use the word prisoners. Due to some legal fuss.

There was one, sometimes two, Somalis in each wooden cell who were all equipped with a blanket and on later trips also a Koran, because someone thought having those would show some class for our part.

The detained pirates received meals three times a day, without pork, and went on a daily walk on the open deck. They were chained together in a long row when they went out for fresh air. We had taken their clothes from them, so they were all wearing some white clothes. It looked quite grotesque, when they staggered past our hangar with the rattling sound of their chains, heading for the deck.

When the cages were full, there were, as far as I remember ten men held captive on Absalon. We got real steel cages on board Esbern Snare in 2010, when we took the seven men from the skiff in the Gulf of Aden in cooperation with the Japanese.

It looked like something from Guantanamo.

While NATO contributed warships, it was the UN's task to find out how to prosecute the detained pirates. It could not be done in Somalia, and most NATO forces would not take responsibility. What sense would it make if a Somali pirate who had tried to attack a Russian ship with a Filipino crew suddenly went to court in a Danish courtroom and went to a Danish prison?

Instead, diplomatic forces worked on making some of the countries around Somalia take responsibility for the legal aftermath. However, that too was a mess. At one point, Denmark, among others, entered into an agreement with Kenya that said we could drop pirates off there. But the agreement was dropped again before we had a chance to make use of it. At one point, the Americans began to transport pirates to the United States, where they were given a trip through the US legal system and ended their days in an American prison. But only if they had seized an American ship or an American crew. Several years later, at the end of my time in Africa, the Seychelles said yes to prosecuting the pirates we detained.

But here, in the fall of 2010, we basically had no plan for the men who sat uselessly in the cages. For that same reason, we did the only thing we could: Under cover of night, the frogmen sailed the pirates to the coast and dropped them off while we hovered in the Lynx above them and made sure everything went as it should. As if that wasn't enough, every pirate even got 100 dollars, so they were able to pay for some food and the trip home after we had dropped them off.

100 dollars goes a long way in Somalia. The pirates must have thought we were idiots. And they actually laughed, when we dropped them off on land. The same men who had tried to shoot us a few days or weeks before. In times like that, you sometimes envied the Russians. The Russians were so tired of the fact that no one would take the prisoners they had, so they just put them into some small motor boats a few hours from the coast. And, from what I heard, only with enough fuel for half an hour.

During the days or weeks the prisoners sat on the ship, the military police interrogated them. They took fingerprints and photographed the suspected pirates in an attempt to make a real data base with our opponents.

How the Somalis reacted to it varied greatly. At one end of the scale, there was the 15-year-old peasant boy who had just taken a chance and was now terrified of what would happen to him. Many of his kind had never seen white people before.

The leader of a pirate group was, on the other hand, typically a hardcore guy who did not respond to questions and consistently resisted or made obscene gestures at the female ratings.

The military police usually handled those types roughly.

The Gazelle, my friend from the Frogman Corps, often assisted the investigators from the military police and helped as a prison guard. He got some good stories doing that. But if you want to hear those, you have to go to Amager in Copenhagen. He has a hot dog stand there today.

I never got much experience with the prisoners we took during my time on the sea off Africa. I liked to stay away, both from the cages on the flex deck and when they came rattling up the stairs on their way to get some fresh air. Of course, I acknowledged that we had an ethical responsibility towards them, and I often tried to remind myself of how we had learned at the Defence College that sailors were sailors, and sailors stick together. The moment a fight died down, we had to treat our opponents with respect, even though they had just tried to kill us, the teachers had said to us.

But, frankly, it annoyed me that we had to behave so relatively decent towards pirates who did not fight for anything other than mammon and who had just shot after us. And I became angry if I was reminded too much about it.

I had no collegial relationship with the people we were fighting against. They were notes in a report and numbers on a piece of paper. Numbers that I kept a close eye on. I had to keep track of when to paint the helicopter.

8. Quest

Okay, old chap, we're rolling again!

In early 2010, Scott and Jean Adam boarded their 58-foot yacht.

Quest, the ship was called.

Since 2004, this married couple had spent their retirement traveling around and handed out bibles in the most remote parts of the world. Scott Adam had worked in the Hollywood film industry and earned a nice chunk of money, and after finding God at a late age, he insisted that his wealth be used for missionary purposes. Part of the savings had gone into the yacht, and together with Jean he had visited such exotic places as Fiji, Alaska, New Zealand and French Polynesia.

With them that day in 2010 were Scott and Jean's best friends, the couple Bob Riggle and Phylis Macay, who were about the same age as them. After all, it was nice to have a company when crossing the oceans.

This time, they were headed for Africa.

In 2011, I was on my fourth trip as pirate hunter.

I had travelled to Salalah in Oman along with HAB, Pylle and our technician Keld Delta, a half crazy but sharp chap from Korsør, who could tame a heavy machine gun like no one else. Along with a bunch of other marines, we were to report for duty on Esbern Snare. We had flown all the way with Emirates and the service had been top notch as always. Pylle and I had watched movies and drunk red wine for most of the trip. Well, until Pylle had fallen asleep and had disturbed half of the cabin with his somewhat fuzzy, high-pitched snoring. The big moustache on his weathered face had vibrated sharply all the while. I had shaved off most of my facial hair, but I had left a perhaps less attractive horseshoe moustache.

Pylle didn't think it was suitable for a professional soldier.

'You should be happy. Every time I do a horseshoe moustache, it doesn't take us long before we get into battle. And you want that,' I replied, laughing.

I was still a little superstitious. I suppose.

We got our passports stamped going into the Salalah airport in Oman – and stamped out again at the harbour a few hours later. As usual, this took place in a back room where you paid the man with the cap behind the desk, who put the money in a cigar box and stamped the passes. I stepped into a bus with the others, and we drove through the large harbour area towards our ship. You could see containers everywhere and a lot of workers who apparently did not care too much about work safety regulations, or maybe safety helmets were just in short supply in these parts.

There was a Maersk container ship in the process of unloading containers using huge cranes on rails. Here, safety seemed to be better, you could tell by the number of personnel with helmets on. Soon after, we arrived at Esbern Snare with its large 5-inch cannon on the front deck. 'L-17' it said on the hull. On the helicopter deck, a large sun canopy had been rigged up to protect the guard from the dangerously strong sunrays.

My own protection against the sun had always been to stay in the shade. 'Pale will prevail,' as I used to say.

There was always a lot of activity around the ship during a harbour stay. Some of the personnel had to be replaced and the ship needed fresh supplies and spare parts. In the midst of this planned chaos, we got a handover briefing from the departing helicopter crew, said hello to the Commander senior grade, the Commander and my old friend Mr Schwann, who once again was the leader of the SMTF-group.

We updated each other about everything at home, and soon it was evening, and the members of the officers' mess, including HAB and me, were invited to dine on a huge cruise ship which was docked just across from us.

We were a beautiful sight in our white tropical uniforms, and the Danish captain showed a clear unspoken recognition for the Navy's clothing style, and many passengers on the cruise ship also got an eyeful.

'Attention all crew on station for leaving harbour,' a voice called out on the intercom the next morning.

I was excited. Quite frankly, I think we were all excited. We longed to open fire in the water in front of some suspected pirates.

As usual, we started with a few training flights with the new helicopter group, as soon as we were out in international waters. It was always a good idea to do some bonding before it got serious. But besides that, it had by now become routine travelling to and from a ship and switch roles between being pirate hunter, husband and father. The ship moved steadily across the blue sea, on a more southern course than usual, through the Arabian Sea into the Indian Ocean. The Gulf of Aden was, nevertheless, already filled with grey ships from various NATO Task Groups and individual countries, such as Russia, China, Taiwan and Japan, who performed specific escort tasks for the merchant ships of their own countries.

Due to this great representation of warships, the Gulf of Aden was no longer as dangerous to the civilian ship traffic as it was a few years earlier. The pirates now had a tendency to move further out into the Indian Ocean with their attack groups, consisting of a mother ship and a couple of fast skiffs in tow. Unfortunately, their professionalism had simultaneously increased, and their navigation back and forth was effectively carried out using GPS with waypoints and routes, all provided to them by the bosses at home in the pirate camps, our intelligence said.

On our flights we met many sailing ships out here on the open ocean. Large and beautiful modern sailing ships which were probably traveling around the world. Some sailed in groups, while others were totally alone. Most were going from India to Oman or vice versa.

We were out to sea many days at a time, so occasionally we had a rendezvous with a supply ship at a given place at a given time. In the Indian Ocean, our ship sailed up next to an enormous naval tanker – in this case, a US supply ship. This procedure was called replenishment at sea, RAS. Soon we were connected to large hoses that provided us with fuel for the ship's large tanks and helicopter fuel for some other tanks. After a while we were "topped off" and the tanker pulled back its tubes and we played our RAS-tune on the outdoor speakers at full volume. It was a pleasure every time you experienced seeing the ships "split up" going at full force forward through the water to the sound of AC/DC.

After 14 days, we still hadn't encountered any of the pirates who were supposed to be in this area according our intelligence. But then one day when we were all just monitoring from the air, looking out over the sea and checking the instruments in the helicopter we saw something. I tried to optimise the radar. When the sea is as flat as it was that day, it is easier to spot small targets such as sailing ships, dolphin flocks and possibly pirate mother ships. There was a good atmosphere, and HAB was actually about to head home to Esbern Snare when I saw a small dot blinking on the screen in front of me.

'HAB, I have a small target on radar with a bearing of 190/15 nautical miles, let's investigate.'

15 nautical miles. 28 kilometres.

Soon we had the target in our sight, and I reported it to Esbern Snare: 'New unknown 1003 in position, tracking 220 speed 7 knots, U1003.'

'Copied U1003, investigate,' the ship replied.

'WILCO out.'

Soon we were able to see a sailing ship on the horizon. A sailing ship with a big dinghy on tow. We continued in order to show him our presence. If nothing else, those on board would have a funny story to tell when they arrived in port. After all, not everyone was lucky enough to meet a fully armed naval helicopter.

'Let's say hello,' I said, smiling. I could see him in my binoculars.

'Yes, sir,' HAB replied and winked at me. Then everything changed.

There was something wrong with the image in my binoculars. There were some black figures on board, I could see.

'Fuck. They are pointing weapons at us. AK-47 and RPG!' I exclaimed.

The mood in the Lynx instantly became acute and intense. No one said anything.

Everyone kept to the procedure.

'HAB, open up, it's pirates, do a big circle around and continue on a western course. Gazelle, are you taking pictures?'

'Plus!'

I called the ship.

'U1003 now suspect 1003, a hijacked sailing boat, name Quest from USA, towing two pirate skiffs.'

We pulled away from them in order to not provoke but before that we had clearly observed at least three white faces. Then I noticed that we had another target on the radar 15 nautical miles north of us. A target that was going the same course and speed as the sailing ship.

We left the sailing boat and investigated the case to the north, and soon we were able to report a dhow to Esbern Snare. It mostly looked like a Yemeni fisherman's dhow, but without visible fishing tackle and with a lot of fuel in the form of oil barrels and no people in sight.

HAB and I were thinking the same thing, I could tell.

What is it doing here and why is it on the same course and speed of the hijacked sailing boat?

Esbern Snare allowed us to pass the dhow to take pictures. A couple of Arabic-looking people came out and waved at us.

Hmm.

Could there be pirates with weapons hiding somewhere? The thoughts were racing through my head, while we already on our way back to Esbern Snare started sending pictures to the experts in the Ops-room, so that they could take a closer look at them.

Investigators on Esberg Snare assessed that we were in fact dealing with pirates here. Both on the fishing boat and on board the sailing ship which according to the pictures had the name Quest and was registered in the US. The plan was to land on the Esbern Snare, out of sight from the fishing boat and yacht, and fuel up the helicopter. When it got dark, we would return and take control of the mother ship, based on one of the top standard plans in the drawer:

Frogmen in the boats with us as the top cover. In the Ops-room, we went through the details of the upcoming mission, then we got a light meal and got ready. We had already talked about it on the flight from Denmark, about having to shoot people if needed. Keld Delta and Pylle had expressed that they were both more than ready for it.

Our contribution to the party was to be in the exact right place, at the exact right time, at any time. We sat there in the dark in our safe, darkened helicopter, only HAB had a minimum of instrument lighting. We were close to the ocean's surface in the dark, and I helped him monitor the height, speed and heeling. Otherwise, I was busy preparing my mono-NVG and getting us in the right position for our part of execution of the plan.

In the back cabin, Pylle sat by the HMG and with his NVGs in front of his eyes. The Gazelle was ready with his sniper rifle, ready to support his friends in the boats below. I had a list on my kneeboard with a time schedule. Some different speeds for variable distances, so I would be able to use our distance from the target to direct HAB's speed. I had coded the direction and distances to the target into to the radar.

The invisible hunter was ready.

'We're going, 285, 60 knots/ I have him clearly on the radar.'

HAB answered in the dark while his eyes scanned his instruments. 'Okay, old chap, we're rolling!'

I checked our timing: 'Get to 100 knots!'

We soon flew with low altitude at 180 kph towards the target. They couldn't hear us yet. But I could hear the Gazelle mumbling in his own patrol radio. He was talking to the other frogs that were racing over the sea with great speed somewhere beneath us.

With the waves we had that night, it must have been a little bumpy. 'Get to 60 knots, one minute!'

We arrived at the scene with our planned entrance: An HMG that emptied its gut on one side of the dhow.

I was sure that Pylle's moustache vibrated vigorously while this went on.

I had turned my focus from the radar image in front of me and over to the left side window and looked out through my NVGs. Pylle ceased fire. It was dark.

Did I see some flashes of light over the sea surface?

Fuck, they shot at us. Luckily, they missed because they had hardly anything but the sound to shoot after.

'Pylle, on my command or by self-defence shoot directly on them,' I almost shouted.

Ten seconds later, the Gazelle announced that the frogs would board. 'Pylle, cease fire, Gazelle will support now.'

It was too dangerous for our own people, if we shot the heavy machine gun while they were on the boat. Instead, the Gazelle took over the air support with his sniper rifle.

Pylle confirmed. I was sitting in a very awkward 90-degree angle with my upper body to watch the scene in my NVGs. I saw several different flashes of light down there and reported back to Esbern Snare.

'Possible firefight, possible firefight.'

I caught myself being a little worried about my friends. Soon after, however, the Gazelle announced that the frogs had taken control of the dhow.

We dragged the pirates' wooden ship around for a few days. Then the miners were allowed to blow it up into small pieces, with great jubilation, of course.

Neither frogs nor pirates were hurt. The moment our people had come on board the dhow, the pirates had put their weapons down. It also turned out that there were only Arabs on board. And there was actually a lot of fishing gear on the boat. As they were obviously following the American sailing boat Quest, we were therefore visited by two agents from the United States. They worked for the NCIS, Naval Criminal Investigative Service, a division of the US Navy which only investigated crimes committed at sea.

As I had been given my own *lukaf*, one of them stayed with me during the days he was there to interrogate the Arabs. He ended up concluding that they were actually fishermen from Yemen but that for some reason they had gone over to the pirates, after being hijacked.

'It had happened several times lately,' he said. 'We cursed a whole lot about that.'

It may sound like a joke. But, so far, it had been important to us that we could count on the black figures on the suspicious boats being pirates, while the rest were not. It had been one of our tripwires. Now we couldn't trust that any more.

The two NCIS agents ended up taking the Yemeni fishermen with them. I don't know what happened to them, but they were perhaps set free again later. At the same time, the Americans took over the handling of the sailing boat Quest, that was still sailing around with the Somali pirates and four American hostages on board.

When the agent from NCIS had left I could enjoy living alone again. It was pure luxury compared to the previous trips when I suddenly didn't have to share a bath and toilet with anyone. HAB had been given the same luxury but in order not to become total hermits, we often met in Pylle and Keld Delta's *lukaf* and had a coke. We also did this on the evening after we had taken the Arabian pirates and their ship.

'It worked again, huh?' I laughed and fiddled with my horseshoe moustache. The others could only agree with me.

Unfortunately, there was not much for Scott and Jean Adam, Bob Riggle and Phylis Macay to laugh about. While the NCIS agents had pulled all imaginable information out of the Arab fishermen, their colleagues had been studying drawings of the sailing ship Quest. They had learned about the habits of the four aging Americans and had gained an overview of their seven hijackers.

At the same time, a Navy SEAL unit had performed an investigation and planned a mission to free the hostages.

One night, shortly after I said goodbye to the agent from NCIS, they attacked. Before that, the pirates had fired an RPG against the American warship following Quest. The soldiers from the Navy SEALs replied by shooting at the pirates. Apparently, two of them were hit by snipers and killed on the spot, while two others were killed when the soldiers shortly after boarded the sailing ship.

By that time, Scott and Jean Adam, Bob Riggle and Phylis Macay were already dead.

The three remaining pirates had executed them when the Americans attacked. Two years later they were all sentenced to lifelong imprisonment in the United States.

9. Ing

Those assholes better keep their hands away from our children.

A naval ship underway moves in so-called maritime speed, where fuel consumption is not exponentially exaggerated. You get used to the speed and the vibrations it creates in the ship.

One afternoon we sat at the helicopter office and shared some cake that HAB had acquired in the cafeteria. We talked about everything and nothing. Keld Delta was a little sad that HAB had the clear lead in being "master of farts". Keld was not exactly a novice when it came to passing gas but had met his superior in HAB – especially when we had had cabbage for lunch.

Yes, men of all types are childish. The helicopter office, which was normally used for planning and briefing, became more and more like a trailer office where the young apprentices sat and chattered. And the master's stench hung like a victorious trophy everywhere in the room.

'Well, Keld,' Pylle said to his second technician.

'It took some years to find a superior but you've been kicked off first place.'

We laughed and stuffed ourselves with cake. The noblemen of the sea. Then the walls started vibrating and you could feel that the ship was gaining speed.

HAB and I looked at each other. Something was going on. I got up and walked in a hurriedly, curious trot up through the ship to find out what was going on, through the long, deserted corridors with the many hatches to end up behind the blue curtain in the Ops-room.

The battle information ratings at the consoles looked tense as they sat there and monitored radar systems and other sensors. An intense and serious conversation was going on by the CO's chair where the Commander and the Operations Officer were standing together with Mr Schwann. Their faces were lit up by the light from the screens. I moved through the dim lighting, past whiteboards, computers and flat screens over to them.

'Is it something serious?' I asked. Mr Schwann nodded.

It was February 24, 2011.

Half an hour later, I could brief the rest of the helicopter crew. A Danish sailing boat had been hijacked a few days from our position. "Ing", it was called. A family from Kalundborg. Jan Quist Johansen, wife Birgit Marie, the children, 13-year-old Naja, 15-year-old Hjalte and 17-year-old Rune and the crew members Viktor Greir and Rane Lund. The family had sailed from Denmark back in August 2009, and the plan was to return to Denmark in the late summer of 2011 after two years of sailing. 'No!' Pylle exclaimed.

'Fuck, well...we have to save them!'

We all agreed. The feeling of national pride was sometimes difficult to dig up at home, but here, we were hit by it like a hammer. Danish children! I thought of my own two girls. I wanted the best for all children in the world. Children everywhere should be allowed to grow big and beautiful without being let down or deserted. Our emotions were overwhelming and uncontrollable.

'Those assholes better keep their hands away from our children,' someone said.

'No mercy. Those pirates have it coming,' another said.

During the next few days we made plans. Military plans for the liberation of the hostages. It was our mission, our justification for existing.

What if the pirates got high on khat and went crazy on the sailing boat? We would be ready.

As far as I remember, it took us 24 hours before we were near Ing. At no point did those on board the sailing boat know we were there. By day, we positioned ourselves far away, at night, we moved closer and looked at them with night gear.

Typically, there were two or three people on the deck of Ing, we could see. You could see a white face by the steering wheel of the boat. There were black people standing around him.

Several other tripwires were also present: ladders, oil barrels with fuel. And Ing was heading for the coast, we could see. It was only a question of time. If Ing reached the coast, it would be almost impossible for us to free the hostages. In any case, it would take time, require a lot of planning and some completely different orders from a higher place.

The plan, therefore, was that we should prepare a liberation mission that could be carried out if freeing of the hostages had not been possible in other ways. Or if we received intelligence about the pirates suddenly starting to execute the family members from Kalundborg.

The terrible fate of Quest still haunted us.

We also didn't know if the pirates would perhaps rape some of the women. The intelligence of other countries reported that the Somalis certainly did not hold back when it came to sexual assaults. The daughter in the family had not even reached puberty yet.

During the first 24 hours after the alarm, we sat in a room with drawings. We had already had teams out on reconnaissance trips in the dark of the night and the frogs had quickly formed a pretty good image of where on the sailing boat the hostages stayed. They also knew how the pirates were armed. It turned out that the father on the ship was more courageous than most in these situations. From a computer on the ship, he had succeeded in sending several e-mails to his brother, who passed them on to the Danish intelligence service. He had even been smart enough to write the messages in code, so the pirates couldn't just run them through Google Translate, if they discovered what he was doing.

Therefore, we also knew that the pirates did not have the slightest idea of how to operate a sailing boat. The pirates' navigation skills consisted of a handheld GPS with an arrow showing the direction.

That's why there was always a Dane on the deck.

A day after those vibrations in our ship had sent me off towards the Ops-room, we had a plan for how we should solve the first hostage-taking of Danish tourists in Somalia.

The helicopter crew, the frogmen, the ship's officers and an intelligence officer were there when Mr Schwann outlined the plan: The frogmen were going to attack from two rubber boats at night. We had to arrive simultaneously in the helicopter and shoot on one side of Ing, while the frogs climbed on board from the other. The sound of a heavy machine gun is a terrible noise. You get frightened when you hear one, no matter how tough you are.

The element of surprise was important. The only thing the pirates would be able to hear was the helicopter and before they figured out why, the fire of Allah would come down upon them from heaven. The frogmen had a precise plan for who were going to disarm who out of the seven pirates and how it should happen. We figured there would be three pirates on the deck. The was so little space on the ship that several of the frogs who were to enter the cabin planned to overpower the pirates with knives.

One of them was my friend, Jørgen. He was the first man to kick in the door of the cabin and attack.

As soon as the attack was underway, Pylle would cease fire. Instead, the Gazelle from the Frogman Corps had to take over with his sniper rifle. He was supposed to protect the frogmen against pirates they couldn't see, and make sure no one got the idea to shoot at the helicopter. We did, however, have bulletproof vests on and the floor in the bottom of the Lynx had been reinforced with bulletproof Kevlar, so it could withstand even powerful projectiles. But still.

In fact, the plan was a lot about the one we had used when we had taken the Arabic fishing vessel two weeks earlier, it was just more detailed. When we had gone through it a sufficient number of times, we went into small groups with our own people to talk about the details. Then we gathered again with the others and went through it all again. Nothing should be left to chance.

Several times during the day, video contact was established with Denmark, where the chief of defence,

General Knud Bartels, sat. He was the connection to the politicians in power, Foreign Minister Lene Espersen and Minister of Defence Gitte Lillelund Bech.

In the end, they were the ones who had to approve the mission.

Commander senior grade Christian Haumann informed the Chief of Defence that we with great certainty were able to free the hostages without any losses.

Our helicopter crew was in a high gear and we were used to operating at night. We had just taken a mother ship and we were confident. The hunter was competent and hungry. Our new work rhythm was now that we primarily were ready for missions at dusk, so it was perfectly fine to slumber in the bunk during the day with a flight suit on, of course. At one point, Pylle and I were looking at a picture of the hostages.

'Henrik, those children and the others just have to get to safety here with us!' I could only agree.

That afternoon, Mr Schwann came by to hear if we were prepared for the liberation mission.

I looked him straight in his eyes. 'We're ready,' I said.

'Good,' he said.

'Because we're picking them up tonight.'

That evening, we walked across a dark helicopter deck to the awaiting Brumbass. You could just slightly detect the HMG sticking out of the left side and the Gazelle pottering around in the cabin to check his equipment. I had had a plate of bulletproof Kevlar installed in my side door and the floor had also been prepared. I met Basse on the deck, a big blond deck rating who in Viking times would have had a long fork beard under his horrifying helmet with nose protection and a huge double-edged axe in his hand. He was putting down the safety nets around the helo-deck.

'Hey, Henrik, give 'em hell,' he shouted.

'Hey, Basse, you better believe it,' I replied.

On a night like that, I experienced some very changeable feelings. I got in and buckled up. I had asked the Virgin Mary to pray for us when I was in our changing room ten minutes earlier. Now I was strapping on my kneepad with my table of timing of our presence on my thigh.

It was Danish children, for God's sake.

When you fly in the dark, you can't see a thing. We have spotlights on the helicopter but we don't use them because then the enemy can see us.

We have NVGs on our helmets. Those that make us see the world in green. We fly with those on, if the Lynx is prepared for it. This means, there can't even be the slightest dazzling light. Ours were not prepared for it, and therefore we had to fly in darkness.

The air and water were pitch black. We had a radar altimeter so we could see how far we were from the water surface and we had the ship that could tell us what other traffic there was in the air. One time, I also tipped our radar so I could see the air traffic myself, and that is something you should never do, if you are the nervous type. The airspace was filled with American drones that could easily smash our tale if they went off course.

Besides that, we found ourselves in a safe environment in Brumbass that night yet again, ready to start up when we got the order. Ing was out there in the dark somewhere, unsuspectingly heading for Somalia.

It was a little difficult to move in the narrow cockpit with the bulletproof vest under the lifejacket, and the survival equipment and the gun as well. It was quiet on the dark helicopter deck. You could hear a rating from the lashing crew cough in front of us over by the closed hangar door. The Commander's face lit up by the red light up in the Flight Deck Officer cabin.

My inner voice said *come on, let's get this done. Let's wake up Brumbass and fly out into the darkness and meet our destiny.*

Then the radio made a noise.

'Abort, we are stopping the mission.'

'Sorry, what? 'Repeat?'

'Abort, we are stopping the mission, the politicians are saying no.'

Five minutes later, we were sitting in the helicopter office without our equipment, wearing only our flying suits, trying to take in the rather unknown feeling of being stopped in the process of performing our craft by some people who were thousands of miles away. We hadn't exactly seen that one coming.

I got the impression that it was Lene Espersen, who was the boss, who had said no. At least, that was I heard from above.

The mission was too dangerous, the reason was. It was bullshit, I thought.

Our risk analysis was in place. Sure, it was dangerous to be near armed pirates who had nowhere to escape, but our protection would have been Pylle with the HMG and Gazelle with his rifle. I would have been comfortable until otherwise disproved. The frogs would have been alright out there, and we would have gotten that family out.

The next day we all met again.

Ing was still on the way to the Somali coast, and if there had been negotiations, they certainly hadn't led to anything. The intelligence also said that the hostages were being treated badly. I assume that the father on the ship had emailed his brother again.

We continued the video conference calls with the top military leadership in Denmark.

'Probability of success is now 95 percent,' Commander senior grade Haumann told General Bartels.

The frogs had gone through more material and now felt even more sure that the mission could be accomplished without loss of human lives.

Ninety-five percent. It was the highest likelihood of success and the lowest risk of the opposite you ever gave in a military situation.

Commander senior grade Haumann had to repeat his assessment several times, because the video connection to Denmark was bad. The image on the screen flickered and the sound crackled. HAB and I bowed our heads a little while our boss complained.

We had been preparing what we should do in case someone was injured during the mission and had therefore started downloading a large amount of route maps to the closest hospitals in Oman on the computer. It took its share of the bandwidth.

When picture and sound returned for a while, Bartels was clearing his throat back home in Denmark.

'I'm talking to you now, Schwann. What is the probability of doing this without loss of human lives?'

'I also believe it's at 95 percent now, General,' the head of the SMTF-group announced.

'Good. That's what I want to know,' the general said.

'Then I recommend the politicians that we try again tonight.'

Hail Mary, full of grace – the Lord is with thee. Blessed art thou among women, and blessed is the fruit of thy womb, Jesus. Holy Mary, Mother of God, pray for us sinners now and in our hour of death. In the name of the Father and the Son and the Holy Ghost, amen.

That same evening we were back in the helicopter. We had processed the disappointment from the evening before, and I now felt determined while I also feared for my life and my limbs. In the changing room, I had repeated my prayer to the Virgin Mary. But tonight, my prayer had been more intense than the night before. Tonight, we would carry out the rescue mission. Ing was about to reach Somalia, and this was our last chance to play a role in the rescue before it reached the coast.

From the back of the cabin, Pylle again expressed what was in my thoughts. 'Phew, it'll be good to get them over here on the ship. Then I am going to spoil those kids rotten!'

HAB nodded with a concentrated expression in the dark. As usual, the Gazelle sat in the darkness of the back cabin and mumbled into his radio. He was speaking to his friends. Basse stood somewhere in the dark with his strong wide figure at the hangar gate. For some reason, it made me feel safe knowing that he was on our team. I was sure he had us in his good thoughts.

I switched on the green light of my lip-light with my tongue, controlled my kneeboard and shone on my bulletproof plate by my left hand. We were putting our lives in the hands of Pylle and the Gazelle, their self-defence would save us all if the prey snapped at us. We would certainly come within reach of its teeth.

'Starting engine 1,' said HAB, and soon, Brumbass was completely awakened.

We were spinning in the dark on the deck.

The wait felt long, and we used it to do some teasing on the internal and closed communication:

'They would never have made us wait like this if we had brought the rangers. They are the real professionals,' I said.

We were referring to the Army equivalent of the Frogman Corps, the Ranger Corps. A friendly joking remark meant for Mr Schwann and his boys, who we really loved and would do anything for – not least on this evening.

Guaranteed, they were also waiting concentratedly at their post.

'Water?' Pylle asked on our intercom and raised a bottle in the air. That is as far as he got.

'Abort, we are stopping the mission.' It got absolutely quiet.

'What?' We all then shouted.

'Abort, we are stopping the mission. The politicians are saying no again!'

That hit us very hard, it couldn't be true. Why were we even in Africa? If we were not allowed to utilise our skills and solve our tasks – then we could just as well sit at home and

116

watch today's news about the early parliamentary elections and about the conflicts around the world, concluding with a weather forecast for pale people like myself.

I was furious. We closed down, walked in through the hangar into the changing room and took off our equipment. I hung my helmet on the usual hook, so the Jolly Roger skull pointed forward over the visor.

One of the frogs went directly into the ship's gym and ran a half marathon on the treadmill. Yeah, well, that was one way of getting rid of the frustrations. The rest of us just sat in our office.

Damn it.

The rest of the evening and night is a blur in my memories, but I remember the sad breakfast seance the following day with Somalia's east coast out on the horizon. It was, to say the least, not the most cheerful mood I had experienced in the officer's mess room.

At about the same time, Ing reached the Somali coast. We were very frustrated and disoriented on the rest of the trip that year. I don't remember very much from the trip home or the homecoming but I clearly remember getting a slipped disc, which happened after a week in Denmark. I think it was the punishment for sitting in a 90-degree twist in the helicopter during some of the rougher situations where I turned my upper body to the left to monitor the situation down on the surface. Anyway, I was incapacitated and couldn't fly for the rest of the year and I was on a very large dose of painkillers.

It didn't make it easier that the anti-climax with Ing was always stirring around in the back of my mind.

I was angry for months, yes, years, that we were not allowed to free the family from Kalundborg. We should have freed them. It's what I thought then, and it's what I think now.

If we weren't allowed to do it anyway with the sharpness and the experience we had shown we possessed, why were we even there? With the recommendation of the Chief of Defence, from professionals, why did the politicians not want us to do it?

The Americans would have done it without blinking. It was lousy, it was cowardice of the Danish politicians.

Officers like us, we would definitely not vote Conservative anymore, all my colleagues said with a sparkle in their eye, every time I talked to them about the matter. They were also still tired of Lene Espersen. Many of them even had the theory that the Foreign Minister's no was due to the forthcoming parliamentary election. It would look bad for the Minister of Justice, if Danish children were killed on her watch. And I could only agree with her on that. But I'm sure, we would have freed them without loss.

The Quist Johansen family was held hostage by Somali pirates for 197 days. They had been well aware that it was dangerous when they sailed towards the Arabian Sea. The Navy's Operational Command had advised against the journey, but it still did not stop the family from taking that route.

Their plan had been to sail towards Oman, and in the cargo, they had both a shipwreck plan, a pirate plan and a clear strategy. For example, they removed the radar reflector and they sailed without the lantern at night. They also put out fake traces of their position on their website.

Seven days after a stop in the Maldives, they were, however, still attacked by pirates. First they saw a fishing vessel on the horizon that put a motor dinghy in the water, the father later explained. Then they launched their pirate plan.

The 17-year-old son Rune hid the navigation computer, which contained their diary and pictures. 15-year-old Hjalte threw a fishing line in the water, hoping it would get into the pirates' engine. The mother Marie sent an emergency signal over the radio. One of the sailors threw a transmitter in the water that would be able to show that the ship was in distress and where it was. Everything while the father, Jan, steered the boat away from the attacking pirates.

Their plan almost succeeded. The family was taken hostage, but the distress signal was intercepted, and shortly after, we were interrupted in our cake eating.

After 10 days of captivity, the family was commanded to go on board the Greek ship Dover which had also been hijacked and anchored at the beach with 24 hostages on board.

They got their own cabin, which they were allowed to close the door to at night, because of the women in the family. The pirates threatened to kill them daily but each time they ended up breaking into laughter when the family had become sufficiently scared.

The pirate leader told them at one point that the fear of NATO was the only thing that actually kept them from shooting anyone.

Marie Quist Johansen and her 13-year-old daughter Naja wore Somali clothing and were not allowed to speak directly to the men.

The long and difficult negotiations to free the family were between the pirates and Jan Quist Johansen's brother home in

Denmark. During July, the parties supposedly agreed on a ransom, and during August, the family's relatives managed to gather the 16 million DKK which was the price for the family and the two sailors.

The insurance money from the family's sailing boat Ing was included in the ransom. At that time, the sailing boat had drifted away and was later found by an American warship that, in agreement with the insurance company, blew it up, because towing it to land was not worth it.

On September 6, the family Quist Johansen and the two sailors boarded a dinghy with an outboard motor, which they had to sail away in themselves. Shortly after, they were picked up by an American warship.

As far as I know, the Frogman Corps had a plan ready, so that the Quist Johansen family could be freed from their prison on the ship Dover if needed. But activating it had probably been far too dangerous.

I don't know much more about what happened to the family, other than what I have read in the newspapers – or heard from colleagues who regularly followed the family's situation. So, I don't know how they are doing today. But I hope they are happy to know that we were many who thought about them and were ready to save them, if we had been allowed.

10. Corpse in the Cargo Hold

There, there, little OBE, it's gonna be alright.

Where the year before had been characterised by a lot of action, 2012 was a quieter period for us helicopter boys. That didn't mean it was quiet for the rest of the ship. Quite the opposite.

But the boring stuff first: Our aging helicopter type combined with a strained spare part situation made us spend a lot of time on the ship, instead of in the air. Our otherwise faithful Lynx spent a lot of time in the hangar.

It was grounded, as we called it. That means, it wasn't allowed to fly. Of course, we could have taken advantage of the situation by dilly-dallying on a state-paid cruise, but the truth was that it didn't feel good to be useless on a naval ship. You felt excluded from the game.

One day there was a parking ticket in the window of the Brumbass which had been standing for a few days in the hangar. The ticket looked real with its greenish colours and in its small plastic chart. It was properly made out with Brumbass' VIN number and was, I must admit, a funny input to an otherwise boring everyday life.

Before we got the ticket, we had, however, done a little flying, and the situation at "the Horn" was now that the grey ships had created some peace and quiet. There were significantly fewer hijackings or attempted hijackings. I experienced, on the other hand, that the pirates had become more vicious and eager to point their weapons at us when we finally did meet them. Possibly because of the many militia soldiers who more and more tried their luck as modern pirates.

It was still RPGs and AK-47s, we could see in the binoculars and on the pictures when we got home but every once in a while we also stared at a heavy machine gun. We regularly had reconnaissance flights along the Somali coast to understand the what the situation normally looked like and to follow the developments of the known pirate camps. And sometimes we passed hijacked merchant ships that were anchored close to the coast. We didn't fly as close to those any more, as in the beginning of the task force. It was revealed on some of our earlier photos and pictures that the pirates on board shot after us from inside the bridge. With knowledge of that, there was no reason to challenge fate more than necessary.

Several tankers and container ships had begun to sail around with pirates on board instead of just lying and functioning as hostages by the shore. The larger ships made it possible for them to sail further from the Somali coast. It had helped them to expand their hunting grounds which now stretched as a triangle from Yemen and Oman in the north to the Seychelles, Tanzania, Madagascar and Mozambique in the south and India in the east. A team of pirates had set a record in February 2011 when they attacked a tanker just 40 nautical miles from the coast of India, about 1,700 nautical miles, or just over 3,000 kilometres from Somalia.

For the pirates, there were also other advantages to using the large merchant ships as mother ships. They then got access to radars and other communication equipment, which they had learned to use. The radar could tell them where other merchant ships sailed and steer the mother ship towards them.

All in all, Somalia's pirates were better organised and heavier armed and better at developing their tactics so they could handle the countermeasures the shipping companies and the international fleet set up for them.

A Somali pirate group consisted of a leader, a team of pirates and one or more investors. Typically, the most experienced pirate was automatically the leader. He took a larger slice of the cake than the others but he also had the responsibility of obtaining fuel, weapons, food and a ship if you didn't have one already. The investors behind him made sure he had money for all of this. It was often former pirates who wanted to invest their ransom in new pirate attacks, or just ordinary business people who had spotted a good investment.

When the leader had found his financial backing, he put together his team of pirates. He needed people who were good at operating weapons, some who were good at sailing, and some who could repair ships, cook and navigate. As there came more serious investors after 2010, the pirates also had more money, better leaders and more professional soldiers he could choose from. The number of hijackings were now reduced, but those that did happen were more severe and more successful than before.

The pirates had simply risen to the occasion.

For the same reason, we were also very cautious when, after some weeks, we got Brumbass flying again and, as one of the first tasks, made a photo reconnaissance of a hijacked Iranian trading dhow, which was obviously being used as a pirate mother ship. Management on our ship were also cautious, and instead of sending us along with the frogs, we were ordered to put the helicopter in the hangar and retreat to the ship's starboard side just like the majority of the rest of the crew. The port side, where our helicopter office was, was then taken over by the frogmen. And then Esbern Snare sailed up next to the Iranian trade dhow while the frogs opened fire.

We stayed all afternoon in our dressing room on the starboard side where an RPG grenade would cause the least damage. While we sat there waiting, we talked a little about how we had seen the hostages on the trade dhow stacked together on the front deck, while the pirates hid in the wheelhouse and elsewhere.

Late in the afternoon, the sound of shots died out and we were called back to our regular posts. The pirates on the Iranian trade dhow had surrendered and the military police were now busy getting them registered and filling up the prison.

The former hostages, on the other hand, were given residence, some food and water and the opportunity to call home. They were also allowed to move around accompanied on the ship, primarily to get some fresh air on the deck while we headed for the Seychelles to drop them off.

When neither we nor the liberated hostages could still fully enjoy the situation that day, it was because one of the Iranians had been hit by a bullet during the liberation mission.

I thought it was weird that we were allowed to go so close to an Iranian ship without a plan that had guaranteed success, while we wouldn't even dare to approach a Danish sailing ship. We had pushed the pirates, there was no doubt about that.

Without specifying which manager authorised that action, I got the impression that some of the crew members had not considered the chance of success as high as he had.

The body of the Iranian was moved to Esbern Snare. It was by no means the first time we sailed around with dead people. We had previously experienced that both pirates and hostages had been dead when we boarded a ship without us having anything to do with it, as far as I was informed.

We put the bodies in a freezer on the ship. If it were a hostage, we brought him to port so that his family could have his body if it was possible to find them. The pirates, on the other hand, got a so-called burial at sea. When we did this, one of the other prisoners typically read something from the Koran, after which we rolled the body overboard.

Fortunately, I never experienced any of our own soldiers being killed or seriously injured during our actions. The closest we came to that was when one of the frogs was hit by a projectile in his helmet.

*

Not long after our fight against the Iranian ship, our Lynx was grounded again. There were new engine problems. This time we decided to not let it bother us, but tried instead to find a common hobby.

Non-original as we were, it ended up being the card game Hearts.

'Aaaaargh,' OBE shouted every time he got a bad hand. 'There, there, little OBE, it's gonna be alright,' Pylle responded.

Bjarne and I were constantly trying to maintain our poker faces. We were benched around the table in the helicopter office playing Hearts, day in and day out, while the technicians worked on the Lynx. The daily ritual with drinking morning coffee and playing cards added new meaning and importance to our everyday lives. When Pylle had a good hand, his moustache always began to vibrate and quiver a little while the rest of his face was as made of stone. Bjarne, on the other hand, was completely unreadable and unpredictable, a complete madman. I even trained the game in secret on our authorised Hearts-simulator in the Windows package, where I named my opponents OBE, Pylle and Bjarne to make it as realistic as possible.

Another one our pursuits to fill the time was Bjarne's so-called group therapy. His idea was that it would solve the tensions we got from drifting idly around.

'What's bothering you?' he asked.

He was deeply serious and had the best intentions. But marines do not have immediate access to their feelings that way.

'OBE snores violently, despite the fact that I put nose clips on his bedside table for him,' I replied.

'You are such a light sleeper, you're not tired enough in the evening after your afternoon nap,' OBE retaliated.

The therapist had to surrender and play along:

'Calm down, OBE, is there something you need to get off our chest?'

'Hey, it's my turn to talk now. I feel that OBE's and my relationship is in crisis, he doesn't speak nicely to me anymore,' I interrupted.

Right then, Gartner came into the office and seemed, as usual, in full balance with himself, despite training hard all morning. Only a slightly raised eyebrow revealed his curiosity towards the office process. He sat down in the soft blue sofa under the large map of the sea area by Somalia and sipped his coffee.

Pylle now interfered loudly in the conversation: 'Bjarne, you make such a mess of our *lukaf*.'

Bjarne tried to keep the last remaining control.

'Quiet, one at a time,' then OBE broke in on the conversation again:

'Henrik says he has fantasies about you, Bjarne,' he proclaimed before everyone just burst into laughter.

Okay, you probably had to be there.

One month later, at the end of March 2012, we sat at a beach bar in the Seychelles and toasted. We were going home to Denmark that night. We were in our last group therapy and certainly not the first drink.

The issues that had been heavy on me in 2008, both before I left, and when I got home, had now become routine. For example, I don't remember that I debriefed with a psychologist, as it was otherwise mandatory in the beginning.

Later, it has occurred to me that, in fact, that was a red flag. That there is just as much need for a psychological debriefing after the fifth voyage, as after the first. But my attitude had become too routine, and I convinced myself that I didn't need that sort of thing.

When I came home to Denmark that year, we moved again. This time from the forest and into the city. Silkeborg, my birthplace. And in August, Lisa gave birth to Gustav. We were all happy about the new addition to the family, also my two daughters, Sofie and Laura, who now became proud big sisters. I safeguarded Lisa and Gustav around the clock – only interrupted by a month's NATO exercise in the Mediterranean in mid-September that year. I had homesickness the whole month the exercise lasted.

When I returned home, fortunately, I had time to enjoy the family before heading to Africa again in the beginning of December.

It was hard saying goodbye to Lisa with our little Gustav in the pram, three months old. For the first time, she was nervous that something should happen to me.

On my way to Copenhagen Airport, I stayed with HAB, who was going the same way. He lived with his girlfriend in Roskilde. In the evening I had to quietly promise her that I would take good care of HAB.

She was also nervous, I could feel.

Two days later, we arrived in Oman, where Esbern Snare was in port. We arrived just as the off-duty part of the crew were having their Christmas lunch. An extremely excellent way to test my new promise to Our Lord that I would no longer drink alcohol.

Over the years, I had slowly built up an unhealthy relationship with alcohol, and I realised that I was using it to escape some of the concerns I had in my head. I was young in the 1980s, and I watched on TV how John Wayne tackled his human problems – by emptying a bottle of whiskey.

I had imitated that image for many years.

Both HAB and I checked into our cabins and then joined the festivities. He with a beer, I with a soda.

But not many months went by before I really needed a drink.

11. The Ops-Room

No, it can't be true!
We're not going over land, are we?

On January 12, 2011, the longest hostage situation in the history of Denmark began. A group of Somali pirates crawled aboard the bulk carrier MV Leopard in the Arabian Sea, close to the coast of Oman. The ship was owned by the Danish shipping company Shipcraft. There were six crew members on board, four Filipinos and two Danes: the Chilean-born captain Eddy Lopez and his mate, Søren Lyngbjørn.

As had also been the practice during the hijacking of the sailing boat Ing, authorities made the public hear as little as possible about the drama while it was going on. All experiences said that media coverage could risk pumping the ransom up and thus prolonging the situation. During 2012, Ekstra Bladet unfortunately broke the consensus Danish media had about not mentioning the hijacking. The newspaper thought that the case was being dragged out unnecessarily and that not enough was being done to free the six hostages. With the headline 'Are Søren and Eddy going to rot in Somalia?' Ekstra Bladet launched a large-scale campaign that would put pressure on both the politicians and the shipping company. The newspaper pushed hard with their campaign, which especially went after the shipping company and its unwillingness to pay a ransom and there were several demonstrations at the town square to get the attention of the people in charge.

Although I hadn't been in Africa when MV Leopard was hijacked, I knew a lot about it because of a phone call I received one day in my home in the woods by Silkeborg.

The next day, I participated in a meeting at the Defence Command in Copenhagen. At a secret meeting, I was briefed on the case, on the development of the negotiations, which at that point had reached a standstill, and on the situation of Eddy Lopez, Søren Lyngbjørn and of the four Philippine crew members.

Søren Lyngbjørn was seriously ill, said the intelligence. It might therefore be necessary to use force in bringing the hostages home.

In the days to come, I sat with representatives from, among others, the Frogman Corps and Hunter Corps and planned how the six men could be liberated. Our task was to make a so-called emergency plan, which could be brought forward, if we suddenly got information that Søren Lyngbjørn was dying in his captivity in the Somali wilderness. We quickly concluded that there were two ways to approach the Somali pirate camp: from the water or from land. We searched for an interim runway in the desert, where a Hercules aircraft could land and drop off vehicles with special forces and at the same time we planned that an attack group consisting of frogmen or hunters could enter the jungle from the sea side and fight their way 15 kilometres into the land where the hostages were located.

My task was to lead a helicopter in providing the soldiers with support from above.

It was a good plan we made during those days, I thought. Good, but of course also risky. Fortunately, it was never launched.

Not that I forgot about Eddy and Søren, as Ekstra Bladet accused the shipowners of. But as I said, I was busy with other things: We moved, got Gustav, I dropped the alcohol, went on a posting during Christmas, returned home and figured that I would take some time off. Maybe go on paternity leave like a true modern man.

But it was not to be.

On a Friday in the end of March, I received another phone call.

'Do you remember Søren and Eddy?' My boss asked at the other end of the line. Eh, yes, those weren't names you forgot in the pirate hunting profession. The two Danes, along with their Filipino colleagues, had been detained for over two years by that time, and the whole of Denmark was gradually acquainted with the matter. It was probably also meant as a rhetorical question by my boss.

'You have to go south on Tuesday. The ship has been extended. You have to go down and get Søren and Eddy out,' he said.

It was my turn to go, and the TACCO who was down there didn't want to stay overtime.

By that time, I was feeling quite used up. Like a worn tool. I had just returned home at the end of January, having been away for Christmas and New Year and I was definitely not geared for travelling to the Seychelles again to report for duty four days later.

'Yes, yes.' I sighed.

Luckily, Lisa was flexible and she almost didn't flinch, when I talked about the phone call with the chief. Only a small crease at the right corner of her mouth revealed that until now I had been pretty absent from her and seven-month-old Gustav. Shortly before, we had also found out that we were expecting another child, seven months down the line, and that did not make the situation less pressured.

'You seem to be taking this awfully well,' I said to Lisa.

In fact, none of us were ready for another child. We were already running on fumes with Gustav who had a stomach ache and also started getting ear pains. In addition, Lisa had problems with her pelvis during her new pregnancy. And me, I was worn and stressed and felt like I never had time off. Now I had four days to prepare for what I expected to be a regular liberation mission.

Not long after, I was in Qatar with MER, Keld Bravo and Bjarne and waited on taking the last stretch to the Seychelles where we had to board the F361 Iver Huitfeldt – Denmark's new warship that had replaced Absalon and Esbern Snare in the Gulf of Aden.

Here it turned out that what we thought was a mission to liberate using force, was instead a situation where the negotiations between the pirates and the shipping company regarding the size of the ransom apparently were about to end. Therefore, Iver Huitfeldt was not going home as planned, but would stay at the Horn of Africa to support the release of the two Danes and the four Filipinos.

It suited me very well. The adventurous spirit that had had me craving action and shooting of pirates a few years earlier was replaced by a more mature feeling. I wanted to solve the task – and then get home and be a father.

We quickly got into the routine on the ship. Luckily, I knew Carsten Fjord-Larsen from my years in the Navy, right from the time I was a cadet and student on his ship Glenten, on to exercises in the Mediterranean in 2004 and the mission at the Horn, where we had encountered one another a couple of times. It was a comfort to have a father figure on board – one you looked up to, and one you knew wanted the best for you.

The first month on Iver Huitfeldt was nice and quiet. We did our mandatory flights, but saw nothing of interest and felt that it was the six seamen being held as hostages on land that had our focus.

After three or four weeks, the ransom negotiations for the hostages escalated. A sum had been agreed upon, we were told, and shortly after, the first money drop was made by a civil aircraft from the Seychelles. The second money drop followed shortly, and at the same time, the time and place for the release of the six hostages was agreed upon.

The agreement was that the Somali pirates would take Eddy Lopez, Søren Lyngbjørn, Frankly Rencio, Sancho Lusaya, Rene Aviles and Federito Nunes to a nearby beach where the frogmen would receive them before we would transport them to the ship in the helicopter.

Until now, there had been no messing around in the pirate industry in connection with the delivery of freed hostages. In the long run, it would be bad for business for the pirates, if you couldn't rely on the details of a release, so we all figured it was just a formality. Although we had never picked up released hostages before, it was as close to routine as it could get. Or so we thought. Right up until April 30, 2013.

'Can you fly into the country and retrieve them?' the boss shouted through the Ops-room.

He looked at MER, the helicopter pilot who had been summoned over the intercom.

'Yes,' MER replied promptly.

I stood next to him and felt the cold sweat all over my body. What did he say?

We're not going over land, are we?

The thoughts were racing through my head.

I had been present in the operations room for some time to follow the development, and it did not look good. There were disturbances in the area, the intelligence said.

Clan disputes.

The money had long since been dropped and counted, and according to the deal, the six hostages should have been on their way to the beach by now. But nothing happened. Nothing had happened for hours. And now, rumours had it that there was trouble on land. Management feared that another clan or pirate group would try to kidnap the hostages. Or that they would get caught in crossfire.

'Can you fly into the country and retrieve them?' MER was cocksure.

Time was running out. The hostages would not be able to be handed over on the beach and time agreed upon.

The darkness was on its way.

Our CO seemed more tense than I had ever seen him before, and the battle information ratings at the consoles were sweating anxiously while monitoring their radar systems and other sensors. The light from the screens painted their faces in a hue of anxiety. I moved through the dim lighting, past whiteboards, computers and flat screens over to the large briefing table where the pictures of the location of the last money drop still lay – a dried-out river surrounded by scrubs.

We were going in there? I became more and more afraid. As afraid as I had never been. Anxiety spread in me. Now I was going to fly into Somalia, get shot down and taken hostage by pirates.

'No, it can't be true! We're not going over land, are we?'

There are very special rules for how to behave, if you are shot down behind enemy lines.

You move at night and you hide during the day. You go to areas that have already been selected from home. You always have a GPS on you, so your people know where you are.

We had been on several combat search and rescue courses. Often, they had taken place on the Jutlandish heaths.

'You have crashed now, goodbye.'

We were thrown out of a helicopter on a wasteland field in the pitch-black night, and then we stood there, two men. Our radio was coded so we could text home immediately.

'We've gone down, we're alive.'

Then we shut the radio off and went to the predetermined designated area. Designated area of recovery.

Where we would be picked up.

In reality, you would of course prefer to stay close to your helicopter and wait for the frogs to pick you up. But this was often impossible. Instead, you had to walk or run, only armed with your gun and a carbine rifle, if you had managed to get one out of the helicopter. Often with half an army or a whole village after you.

It was the Home Guard with their dogs who chased us when we were on a training exercise. When we were finally picked up, after walking many kilometres through the night, one of the most important things was not to appear threatening to those who came and got us. We had to sit with our backs towards the landing helicopter, with our ID card in hand, when the rescue team arrived. If we didn't, we failed the exercise. When they grabbed us, we had to say a pre-agreed code word. Something that only we knew. The name of our mother or dog. Only then were you dragged into the helicopter, ready to fly back to freedom.

It was not like in a movie where you helped freeing yourself by shooting. In the Balkans, an American pilot who had been shot down almost got himself killed, because he was being a smart-ass and ran toward his rescuers holding a gun up in the air.

We had also trained being taken captive.

The most important thing a hostage must do is survive. It is no longer like it was during the Cold War, where only name, number and rank should be mentioned. Nowadays, on the contrary, you have to humanise yourself, the procedure is called. Then it is harder for the captors to hurt you.

If they want a phone number, give them one that connects to the Defence. If they ask if you believe in God, say yes.

But avoid telling them which god. One time, some of my colleagues picked up a boat in the Gulf of Aden with two sailors. They had escaped the pirates, but their two colleagues had been shot. Because they had said they were Christians.

As a hostage, the most important thing is to maintain control of your psyche. You may acknowledge to yourself that you are physically in the custody of the captors but you must never let them get hold of you psychologically. And that is actually one of the most difficult things. For the same reason, we were also on hostage courses in Denmark, where we were essentially humiliated throughout the entire course.

One time, in the Melby camp in North Zealand, I was handcuffed and got a sack over my head. Then I was put out in the rain, only wearing my underpants and boots without laces. It was mid-December. There I stood for almost 24 hours while it was raining, and my captors played some terrible music over and over again. I only sat down the few times I was being questioned or when I managed to convince them that I had to use the toilet.

We also learned how to communicate in front of a camera, before we first went to Somalia.

Before an international mission, we would write down some signs and what they meant. Then we had an agreement with the intelligence service on how we personally intended to show that our life was threatened. For example, I had written down that if I spoke Oxford English, then I was speaking under coercion. If I said my whole name, Henrik Monggaard Christensen, it meant that I loved my family. That could mean a lot to them.

The best thing to do as hostage is to stay in the same place, if you can. So those who are going to save you know where you are. But if your life is threatened, then you must of course try to escape. Therefore, we had also learned to pick handcuffs and we had learned how to tear strips.

Well – we had been through it all, we were well-educated and well-prepared. But everything seemed so pointless, now that it could suddenly become reality.

The pirates were well tired of the blue Lynx helicopter that had been bothering them thoroughly for several years. There was no doubt about that. They would love to catch a couple of us.

'What the hell is this? Look at the picture! They can hide a whole battalion in those scrub without us being able to see it,' I shouted at the Executive Officer and slammed my fist into the table.

I was sweating and my mouth was dry as dust.

Fuck, man, we would be tortured, if we were taken hostage by them. Didn't they get that? My little Gustav at home wasn't even a year old yet, and Lisa had another child in her tummy – and what about the girls? I could hardly bear it.

I went over to the Commanding Officer:

'It's the stupidest thing I've heard in a long time. You have to at least get a top cover helo.'

There was uncomfortable silence in the Ops-room.

It was the first lesson in leading military forces: Always having weapon protection from others when moving into a dangerous area.

You could almost hear people's feet twisting in their boots.

The CO nodded, and we both looked at the situation picture on a screen – the closest friendly helicopter ship was several days away, and on top of that, it was a unit of the EU special forces that we, due to the defence reservation, were not allowed to cooperate with.

Oh, God and Mary.

'We need to get them out, that's my job, and you have to contribute to it,' Carsten Fjord-Larsen firmly said.

No, no, no, cried the voice in my head.

I couldn't handle the idea of having to be held hostage for several years – like Søren and Eddy.

I had never been so afraid before in my life.

12. Søren and Eddy in Somalia

Don't worry.
All we want is money.

It was the mate Søren who had been on guard on the bulk carrier Leopard on January 12, 2011. It was he who had been in charge of the ship, out there in the middle of the sea, several hundred kilometres from land.

Suddenly he had seen something on the radar. A small object, 15 to 17 miles away. Søren Lyngbjørn had changed Leopard's course. Just by principle. But the white dot on the screen did not move further away for that reason. The moment after, it stopped moving. The ship which had followed them suddenly didn't move.

Søren had hesitated for just a moment. Then he had decided to wake up the captain. Eddy Lopez had been down in his cabin relaxing. A six-hour shift could well be felt, even if you were an experienced captain. It was just before five o'clock in the afternoon, when the intercom started howling. Without thinking much about it, he had grabbed a T-shirt, a pair of shorts and a pair of sandals.

He had no idea that it would take a long time before he would wear something else again.

Eddy Lopez and Søren Lyngbjørn had tried to remain calm that afternoon. Eddy had grabbed the telephone and called Birgitte Kørner from Nordane Shipping in Svendborg. The shipping company Shipcraft, who owned the carrier, had outsourced the manning of its ships to Nordane Shipping, where she sat as a crew coordinator.

She had answered the phone immediately.

'We're in trouble. We are being attacked by pirates,' Eddy had almost shouted into the phone, he explained later.

'You have to set off all alarms. Everything possible,' Birgitte Kørner replied. 'And then you have to defend yourselves as best you can,' she added.

Eddy hung up, pressed all the alarm buttons, including the one who automatically alerted the Defence Command in Denmark. Then he grabbed the radio.

'Mayday, mayday. Mayday, mayday,' it now sounded from Leopard. But no one had answered the distress call.

Eddy Lopez later explained that he had tried to do some of the manoeuvres that both he and Søren had practiced the day before. Manoeuvres that might keep the pirates off the ship. By steering the ship quickly from side to side, the two men hoped to create such large waves along Leopard that the pirates would not be able to get close to the ship, or that they might even be knocked over.

But that hope had disappeared a few minutes later.

It was Søren Lyngbjørn who had seen that the pirates' boats were now on the side of Leopard. He could see that there were 12 men in each.

Eddy had cursed loudly, but had been interrupted by the sound of shots being fired.

He instinctively closed his eyes when the pieces of glass hit him in the face.

The pirates had shot directly at the bridge with their AK-47 rifles.

The pirates had sailed all the way up next to Leopard and had thrown their aluminium ladders up the side of the ship. The distance from the water surface to the railing was short on the coaster. Although the pirates had to climb up the side of Leopard which was sailing at full speed, and even though they had to pass the special barbed wire with its many small steel blades, which served as small knives, the first pirate came on board quickly. He had cut up the barbed wire with a large pair of pliers.

At that time, Eddy had grabbed the radio and commanded that the entire crew go down into the engine room. Eddy Lopez, Søren Lyngbjørn, Frankly Rencio, Sancho Lusaya, Rene Aviles and Federito Nunes. Here, the six men had barricaded themselves reasonably well.

The next minutes and hours had been a battle against time for the pirates to gain access to the crew. The moment their machine guns pointed at the crew members, NATO forces could no longer come to their rescue. But if the NATO forces reached Leopard before the pirates reached the fortified crew, the pirates had a serious problem.

In the engine room, Eddy asked his engineer, Rene Aviles, to switch off the engine for the same reason that he had stopped the ship. Leopard could no longer escape the pirates who were already on board, and it was important that the closest NATO forces knew their exact coordinates before the pirates possibly succeeded in stopping the alarms that Eddy had set in motion on the bridge. By turning off the engine in the engine room, the pirates could not start the ship from the bridge. Now they just drifted according to the weather. Only a small auxiliary machine was still running and gave power to Leopard. It was also this machine that gave power to the small radio in the engine room which the crew could use to get in touch with nearby ships. With it, they could announce a possible warship that they could safely board MV Leopard without danger to the crew's life.

'Mayday, mayday. Mayday, Mayday.' Eddy tried several times. But each time, the answer was the same: Complete and utter silence.

The pirates hammered at the door with sledgehammers, and by ten o'clock in the evening, the lower part had started giving in. A black head and a rifle had come in through a hole at the floor. Shortly after, the crew was commanded to leave the engine room. Eddy was knocked unconscious with a rifle butt.

The first day in what would turn out to be Denmark's longest hostage-taking situation had begun.

It had gotten dark over the Arabian Sea, as the crew of MV Leopard again came out into the fresh air. On the bridge, all of the alarm buttons were still flashing. It was only here, in the glow from the red light, that Søren and Eddy had the opportunity to see the pirates properly. There were 24 of them, they counted. Some had bare feet, but most of them were wearing sandals, colourful T-shirts and loose-fitting pants. Some just wore a sort of scarf around their waist instead of pants. They were all thin, both on the bodies and in the faces.

'Now you have me, so don't touch my crew,' Eddy said to them.

The leader of the pirates asked for money and Eddy showed them the way to the safe. Here, they stole 20,000 dollars. Money that belonged to the shipping company and was to be used for cash payments in the ports that the ship passed.

Then Eddy and Søren were asked to start the ship again. But it had broken. During the five hours the crew had been sitting in the engine room, the pirates had tried in vain to bring life to the coaster by pressing, turning and pulling virtually all buttons and handles in the control room, and it had destroyed the machine.

The pirates had to leave the ship, before some of the alerted NATO forces arrived. They had no idea that they really had enough time.

Although we and our colleagues covered a large area, a Turkish warship had been closest to MV Leopard, when Eddy had triggered the alarm, and did not arrive until noon the next day. At that time, Eddy, Søren and the four Filipinos sat in a dungeon under the deck of a worn-out Chinese fishing boat. From there, they were sent on to the Greek ship Polar. A large, old tanker that had been hijacked about two months earlier and now served as a floating prison.

There, the six men spent the next five months and 15 days. They rarely saw daylight and went to the toilet in a bucket.

'Don't worry. All we want is money,' the pirates had repeated, over and over again.

Which, however, was in strong contrast to the fact that they daily threatened Eddy, Søren and the Filipinos with their guns and pretended to shoot, or led a finger across their necks to scare them.

On board Polar, the hostages also experienced how we NATO forces dealt with captured pirates. Three men had stayed on board MV Leopard and had been detained by the Turkish NATO soldiers who had found the ship. But three days later, they came back to their friends. They laughed and patted the other pirates on the shoulders as they talked about how stupid the NATO soldiers had been.

After a couple of weeks in captivity, both Søren and Eddy had called home. To their families and to CEO Claus Bech from the shipping company Shipcraft. Then, the negotiations for their release had begun.

It was customary that the hostages were close to the coast, before the pirates made contact.

As in most other cases, the negotiation of the Leopard men was handled by a negotiator on the coast who was distinguished by being able to speak English.

Every negotiation process had its own dynamics. But in all cases, as in other negotiation situations, it came down finding out who would be the first one to give in and accept the bid of the other.

The pirates gladly started by demanding a high price for the hostages, and the shipping company typically responded with a low bid.

That's how it was with MV Leopard too.

You might think that the shipping companies should just pay the sum that the pirates demand to get the hostages free. Human life is more important than money. But a quick trade and payment can give the pirates the impression that the shipping company has a lot of money, which might make them keep the hostages to push for even more money. It's been known to happen.

Something Ekstra Bladet unfortunately did not take into account when they started their campaign.

Occasionally, it did happen that shipping companies paid high ransoms and got their people free. But that was not unconditionally good either. It had contributed to the price of hostages rising sharply over the years.

In 2005, an average of 150,000 dollars was paid to get a ship and crew set free. In 2010, the sum had risen to 5.4 million dollars.

Instead of paying the high amounts, it was more the tactics of the negotiators to convince the pirates that everything was being done to raise money, but that the company did not have very many. The pirates responded by trying to soften up the hostages' negotiators by stalling for time, so they became worried about the welfare of the hostages. The pirates' negotiators also often tried to make the shipping company believe that the hostages were sick and dying, and that time to find a solution was scarce.

It was like this in the case of Søren, Eddy and the four Filipinos.

The first pictures of the six kidnapped sailors from Leopard were posted on YouTube during July 2011.

They were filmed in a desert landscape, with 15–20 armed men behind them. Søren Lyngbjørn explained that he was feeling ill.

Shortly after recording the message, the pirates moved the hostages into the mainland. Into the interim camp that became their primary Somali home.

In the beginning, the pirates had just thrown five mattresses under some large bushes where Eddy, Søren and the Filipinos had stayed for a few days. Then the pirates had shown some mercy and acquired something that at best resembled a large tent. Later, they also got a small freezer and a generator out in the wilderness. They had also been given a bag with some different clothes and some of the classic Somali dresses that many of the pirates themselves wore, and one of the Somalis had brought some old plastic garden chairs, so that the six men did not have to spend the whole day on the ground among ants and scorpions.

Later, I heard that Søren Lyngbjørn was, however, bitten by a scorpion and during a bizarre session, the pirates had retrieved someone who could best be described as a medicine man. He had, I think, brought both pills and dressings with him, but, in his powerlessness, ended up just spitting on the wound and shouting out some prayers or spells.

It had not exactly helped fight the pain, but Søren Lyngbjørn survived at least.

The six hostages were beaten daily while sitting in their prison camp. And what was worse, the pirates threatened them several times that they would be sold to Al-Qaeda's Somali sister organisation, Al-Shabaab.

Specifically, Shipcraft was told that the sale would happen, if they did not pay 15 million dollars by the end of September 2011.

At that time, Shipcraft offered to pay 800,000 dollars in cash.

In order to give the shipping company one last chance, the pirates decided to record another video. They had heard that parliamentary elections would be held on September 15 and though that the politicians might be more willing to pay due to the upcoming election. In the video, Søren and Eddy repeated how badly they were doing. Eddy had and ulcer, he said. Søren was also ordered to mention the Mohammed drawings. The Somalis wanted to make it crystal clear to the Danish government that they indeed knew about them too. Most likely in order to make the story of the Muslim Al-Shabaab more credible.

As far as I know, the video was never released to the public. But it was sent to Shipcraft and was also seen by people from the Danish intelligence service who at this time had begun to plan what would happen, if we had to use force to get Søren and Eddy out.

However, both the 2011 elections and the pirates' deadline passed without them following through on their threats.

I later heard that Eddy Lopez had asked one of the pirates if the election was over. 'Yes, yes. No problem,' he had just said before he burst into laughter:

'Woman winner!'

Denmark now had a female prime minister, and it was unusually difficult for the Somali pirates to understand.

In 2012, Ekstra Bladet increased its criticism of the fact that Eddy and Søren's situation in Somalia had not yet been resolved, and the pressure on Shipcraft in particular grew immensely. Both the chairman of the shipping company, Sysser Philipson, and the shipping company owner, the extremely rich Swede John Arne Larsson, would regularly see their own names and faces on the front of the papers. The newspaper pointed out that Sysser Philipson went on luxury holidays, while the hostages were sitting in a hole in Somalia, and especially John Arne Larsson was criticised as a leder for not caring about his six sailors. In any case, Ekstra Bladet was able to document that money was in no way missing from his personal money tank.

In July 2012, the newspaper started the concrete campaign that ended up making the Chilean captain and his mate from Ærø nationally famous. 'Are Søren and Eddy going to rot in Somalia?' It said on the 86 square metre banner on the facade outside of the Ekstra Bladets editorial rooms at town square in Copenhagen and on the newspaper's website the hostages in Somalia themselves could keep track of exactly how long they had been captured. A small clock in the corner of the articles made sure of that.

The pirates were obviously happy about the publicity, there was no doubt about that. We heard later that their leader triumphantly came by the camp and showed Eddy and Søren pictures of the articles on his phone. The following winter, Eddy and Søren also had the opportunity to make a statement to Ekstra Bladet. Someone gave Eddy a phone and told him to tell a humanitarian worker on the other end of the line how badly he was doing.

The humanitarian worker turned out to be a Danish-Somali freelance journalist. He had previously made a documentary about pirates in Somalia and had now offered Ekstra Bladet to help get in touch with the hostages. But Eddy didn't know all of this on that warm winter day. He just took the phone and told the same story as he had done so many times before.

'I think they will pay now,' the leader had said afterwards. Shortly after, another of the newspaper's journalists also phoned, among other things to ask Eddy what he thought about Shipcraft's owner allegedly buying himself a house at the price of 55 million Norwegian crowns.

Eddy had almost hung up out of fear. The pirates had more than once made him aware of the fact that they had started recording the conversations and had a man in Denmark who translated them. If they sniffed out too much about how rich the company's owner really was, their demands would just rise again.

The softening began in early 2013.

Specifically, one day when Søren Lyngbjørn was told in half codes from the shipping company to act as if he was even more ill than he actually was. After the conversation, the pirates' negotiator had stricken him, but without full force. It became clear to Søren that the shipping company's negotiator had made an agreement with the pirates' negotiator behind the back of the other pirates. The pirates' negotiator also wanted to close the deal, but to get his friends to agree to it, they had to believe that Søren was dying and thus soon worth nothing at all.

A month later, on April 30, while we were fast asleep on Iver Huitfeldt, Eddy Lopez was awakened. Along with the Filipinos Rene and Frankly. Along with some pirates, they were driven out of the forest, out to a clearing about five kilometres from the camp.

It was two o'clock at night. 'What's going on?' Eddy asked.

'Can you count?' one of the pirates asked him. Eddy had nodded.

'Good. Because now you are going to count money.'

Two hours later, the pirates' phone rang. It was the shipping company's negotiator who wanted to make sure they were in the right position. Another hour later, a small plane flew over the clearing and threw down three large bags from the sky, each of them in a small parachute.

Ransom.

13. Redemption

We have six happy people on board, in route for you.

We were scared.

We were sitting in the helicopter office waiting.

The details of the plan were not clear but we guessed that we would be flying over the mainland with six frogmen in the back.

The six frogmen then had to fast-rope down to the ground, where they were to free the six hostages.

Or, try to.

It was madness.

We were going to be shot down, the frogs would be shot down, while they hung there in their ropes.

What were they thinking? Or maybe they weren't.

Maybe we could just fly them halfway in? We would be discovered anyway. It was unknown terrain. And how were the frogs going to come back with six hostages through the wilderness, and how should we pick them up again?

'It's the stupidest thing we can do,' I said ten times to Carsten Fjord-Larsen.

The man I had seen as a father figure was now sending me to my death. I was angry and scared, angry on the outside, scared on the inside. I didn't care if I was sent home in disgrace. I didn't want to die or be taken hostage by Somali pirates.

Carsten Fjord-Larsen was clearly annoyed that I was opposing. 'I want to help you but I can't,' he said.

Then I left. If I could, I would have slammed the door but the operations room was only bounded by a curtain.

I went straight down and told the technicians, Keld Bravo and Bjarne, what had happened. Bjarne was supposed to come along on the flight and operate the HMG, I figured.

'We can't do that,' he said.

I did not mention that MER had already said yes. I didn't want to expose him like that, and in some way, I understood his decision. You don't say no when you are a professional soldier. I just really didn't want to die.

Fortunately, the situation changed again in the afternoon. The hostages suddenly seemed to be heading towards the coast in a vehicle, we were told. It could just barely be achieved to activate the original plan and get them before dark, where we wanted to avoid going too close to the coast. But it had to happen fast.

Our helicopter group found out that the delay was not caused by clan disputes but by TV2 and Ekstra Bladet who, with the pirates' blessing, just wanted to squeeze one last interview out of the hostages while they were still on Somali soil. I guess the big backers had gotten their share of the ransom and had retreated, and that the peasants in the chess game could not handle the simple task of handing over the six people as agreed upon, probably because they got some extra pennies for setting Søren, Eddy, Frankly, Sancho, Rene and Federito up for an extra interview.

'The hostages have already been waiting for over two years and a couple of months, so what's a few extra hours,' we joked sarcastically out on the ship.

The six hostages had been held captive for exactly 838 days.

But really, of course, we were furious. The Danes apparently had a right to get their breaking news, so the frigate Iver Huitfeldt just had to put its mission patiently on standby, with all the anxiety and chaos that might cause.

In Africa, the sun goes down very quickly and then it's just dark. We had less than an hour after take-off until sunset. We hovered in the air and watched the beach from a distance in order not to make anyone nervous on land there was no time for more delays. After what felt like a long time waiting, we suddenly saw a big dust cloud in the sand, and some Toyota land cruisers appeared. I could see in my binoculars that a group of Somalis holding weapons jumped out and herded a small crowd of people down to the edge of the water. The small, dense group counted six people, and soon they were standing in a line on the shore with their faces turned to the sea. The vehicles disappeared, one after being stuck in the sand, so the pirates had to get out and push it – we somewhat amused by looking at that. Left on the shore were Søren, Eddy, Frankly, Sancho, Rene and Federito.

'They're gone, the coast is clear,' we told the frogs.

We were on an encrypted line and there were no one else with us on the mission, so at this point, we were just speaking Danish.

'Eddy is wearing an orange T-shirt,' I added.

Our order was clear: Søren Lyngbjørn and Eddy Lopez were more important to bring out than the four Filipinos. At that time, I didn't even know their names. It was cynical but that's how it was.

'Roger that. We are on our way.'

The frog Benni told us afterwards that he had sprinted past the six men and into his position in the dunes, from where he was to secure the area.

'We've come to rescue you,' he had shouted as he ran, to the great wonder of the six sailors.

The moment after, the frog's medic, Skrå, had arrived and had examined the six men, and half a minute later Jørgen called us in for landing, and we arrived in a cloud of sand and dust. The six released hostages were accompanied to the helicopter – equipped with ski goggles so they wouldn't get sand in their eyes. Bjarne placed them closely together on the floor of the cabin. We left Somalia and flew the short trip back to the ship, which now lay close to the busy beach.

I turned toward the six now former hostages. Their clothes smelt like smoke from a bonfire. It reminded me briefly of the time when I was a scout. There was a familiar feeling of safety about it, after all. I smiled and gave them a thumbs up, and they smiled gratefully back.

'We have six happy people on board, in route for you,' I reported to Iver Huitfeldt. Back on the ship, Eddy, Søren and the four Filipinos were taken into the hangar in front of us. Here, a larger delegation was waiting, with Carsten Fjord-Larsen in front. There were also doctors and nurses ready. The hangar gate was closed behind them, and we stepped onto a deserted helicopter deck. I paced up to my good friend Claude from Karup, who was on the trip as an intelligence officer. I gave him a USB stick with data from the mission. In return, as bonus information, he told me that TV2 and Ekstra Bladet had gone public with the breaking news of the release, already before we landed on the ship.

I was angry with the boss the following days. Emotions were running high. I felt let down by my father figure. To think, we were so close to being sent into the country on a suicide mission, to fend for ourselves. In reality, the sinners were TV2 and Ekstra Bladet, but they were not present on the ship.

I disembarked Iver Huitfeldt in the Seychelles in the beginning of May a bitter person. My pride as a Marine was hard to locate at that time. I considered leaving the Navy.

During the summer holiday, I read the following in the newspaper Berlingske:

Frigate leader criticises Ekstra Bladet and TV 2 in hostage case.

Commander senior grade Carsten Fjord-Larsen believes that some media were more interested in getting the story out at the right time than in securing the hostages' evacuation, when two Danish and four Filipino sailors were taken hostage by Somali pirates. When Commander senior grade Carsten Fjord-Larsen, on April 30, was waiting for two Danish and four Filipino hostages on the frigate Iver Huitfeldt off the Somali coast, time was, according to the morning paper, Jyllands-Posten, running out. The ransom had been paid, but the hostages did not show up on the beach at the expected time. Carsten Fjord-Larsen received confusing intelligence about a growing threat on land via the shipping company Shipcraft and the Navy's Operational Command from a journalist paid by Ekstra Bladet who was in Mogadishu 500 kilometres away. The frigate commander was therefore close to launching a forceful liberation mission in order to bring the hostages safely out of Somalia.

'The longer the time, the greater the threat to the hostages,' Fjord-Larsen explains to the newspaper.

The hostages were eventually released without a mission being started, but even before the helicopter landed with the hostages, the story was featured as breaking news by Ekstra Bladet and TV2.

'There are strong indications that getting the story brought to the media at the right time was more important for some than securing the hostages' evacuation. Ultimately, it could have meant risking the lives of the hostages, the frogmen and the helicopter crew on the basis of wrong information' Carsten Fjord-Larsen says.

Extra Bladet's news director, Miki Mistrati, denies that the newspaper's journalist should have delayed the release.

'I can say that with 100 percent certainty,' he says.

The frigate commander hopes that the case will remind the media think twice in future situations.

'I hope this case gives rise to an internal introspection in the media about how far you are willing to go in putting other people's lives at risk – and for what purpose. It either points to a high degree of cynicism or a high degree of ignorance,' he says to Jyllands-Posten.

I felt like the commander was addressing me a little bit here – and it felt good.

I hope that we will never again experience extraneous media actively affecting a military operation. When we have a task to solve in the Defence, we prepare our plans with risk analyses, after which we prepare ourselves as best, we can.

Our operations are often dangerous enough as it is, but with a known risk that we recognise and accept working with. We go all in according to the plan.

When TV2 and Ekstra Bladet disturbed the whole plan and created another situation where we were not in control of time and place or knew the scenario on land, then, yes, the military leaders made some decisions that were not optimal in terms of reality and as you know, reality wins every time.

From my tactical point of view, I would also like to encourage responsible politicians, who send Danish soldiers into the world to conduct foreign policy, that they at some point in a given operation they let us military personnel finish the task properly. I am also sorry that we with the fantastic odds in the solid plan we had – were not allowed to carry out a liberation mission on the sailing boat Ing.

This is what we train for, at the taxpayers' expense and we are good at it.

I don't know on what basis the decision to let the family on Ing stay in captivity was taken. But from where I was, on Esbern Snare, it didn't make much sense. Nor have I fully come to terms with that yet.

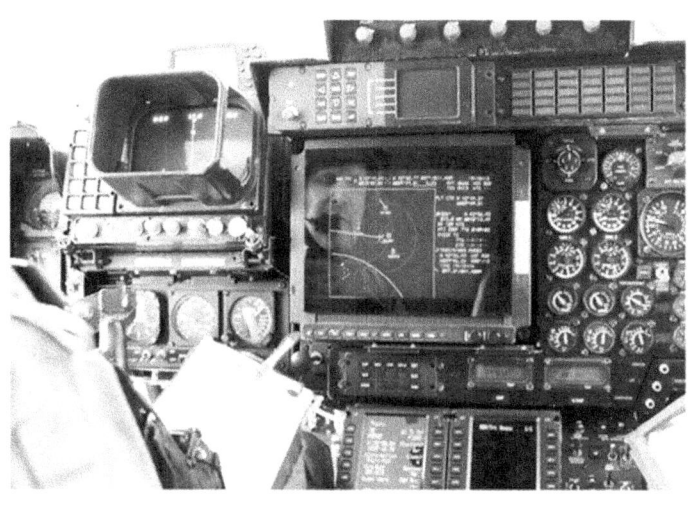

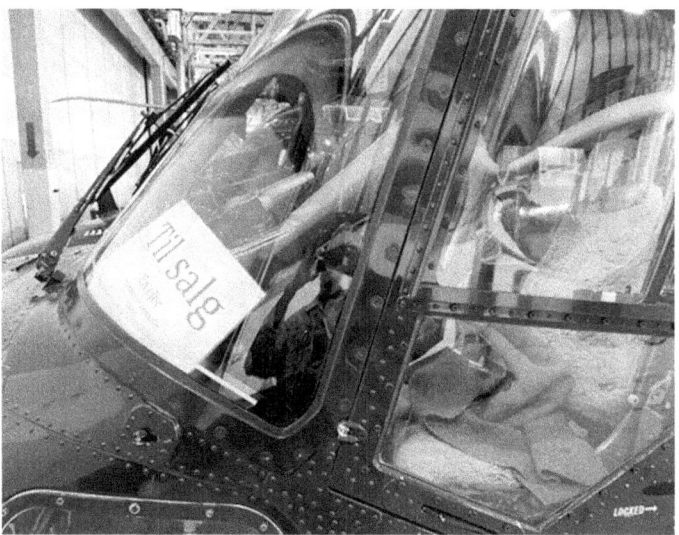

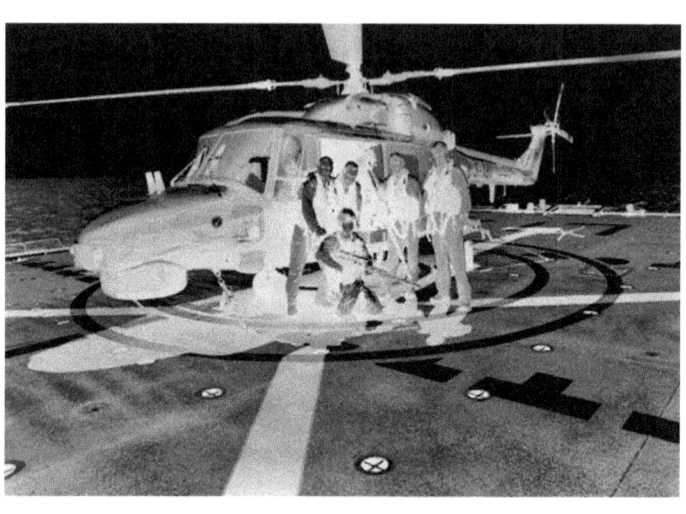

14. Epilogue

Søren Lyngbjørn, Eddy Lopez and their four Filipino colleagues were dropped off at the Seychelles. From here, the two Danes flew with a hospital aircraft to Germany before returning home to Denmark. Today, Eddy Lopez lives in his country of birth, Chile but Søren Lyngbjørn is back on Ærø, where he came from.

Both men are of course marked by the experiences in Somalia, but are also in good spirits and good health.

After the hostage situation, the Press Council expressed their criticism of both Extra Bladet's and TV2's handling of the events. Both Søren and Eddy subsequently filed a case against Ekstra Bladet, who was sentenced to pay DKK 300,000 in compensation to each of the two men.

I came home to Denmark in the early summer of 2013.

Lisa gave me another son. Emil, we named him.

At the same time, there was a break in the Danish efforts against piracy.

Instead, I started doing paperwork at the office in Karup. I also instructed new TACCO students, and I went looking for oil slicks in the North Sea.

A year later, in the summer of 2014, I was diagnosed with depression. I couldn't do shit. I went on sick leave from the service. A lot of the time, I just sat in the bathroom and cried. I hated my life and was not even able to follow my children to their day care in the morning.

It wasn't until one year later, in 2015, I found out with a psychologist that my experiences at the Horn of Africa had given me a real trauma. That half a day when I thought I was going to be sent in to pick up Søren and Eddy had left a deep imprint on me. And the pressure and stress I had been working under in the Gulf of Aden, in an often-hostile environment, had also generally worn me down mentally.

Today, I have succeeded in placing the events in the past. Now I can take them out and talk about them, as I have done in this book. And I can pack them away again.

If anyone feels like details are missing in my narrative, it is due to my obligation of professional secrecy and a thorough efforts not to disclose sensitive information about our work so that future military operations and their participants are not compromised. For the same reason, the names of the different frogmen are fictitious – with basis in reality.

Today, I do not fly a helicopter anymore… Five years ago, I was relocated to the Joint Rescue Coordination Centre, JRCC, in Karup… Here, I was a duty officer, which means I took those emergency calls from 112 that require a boat on the water or helicopter in the air. The cases can be anything from German tourists who have gone our too far in their inflatable bathing rings, to foreign tankers deliberately leaking oil and trying to get away from it.

I was also on duty, when a Swede in the summer of 2017 reported his girlfriend missing, after she had not returned home after a trip with a Danish civilian submarine. It was a busy morning where divers, rescue boats and sonar equipment were required, and where the mood changed continuously: from concern over the missing submarine, to the delight that it was found, to the bewilderment that the missing journalist was not on board.

But that is a completely different story.

After three years in the JRCC, I've been relocated to the Naval Command Denmark, placed in Karup. I now work as a staff officer along with a PTSD diagnosis.

I enjoy my new work, despite my illness. I am working on getting better at controlling my emotions and my temper.

Today, I am again grateful for life and its little miracles, and I have great focus on the good and stable things in my daily life – the boys, the girls, the family, outdoor life and my wife Lene. Lisa and I got divorced in 2016. Our relationship had been worn too far down during the years I was rarely home and mentally lived over the sea off Africa, whether or not I was there.

Today, I am very interested in the conditions of our deployed soldiers, and sometimes worried of whether or not we support them enough, both while they are deployed and when they come home. I hope my story can help put a little more focus on us veterans. There are actually quite a few of us, and we are pretty ordinary people, even though, on the surface, we may seem thirsty for blood and don't seem to be in touch with our feelings.

Soldiers also have parents, siblings, children, wives, ex-wives, husbands and ex-husbands and soldiers also have hopes and dreams, and like all humans, they have a limit to what they can handle.

So, let's look out for of them.